JEWISH NETWORKING:
Linking People, Institutions, Community

Hayim Herring
Barry Shrage

Analysis and Comments
by

David M. Gordis
Allan Finkelstein
Neuman F. Pollack
Alan Silverstein
Christopher Winship
Jonathan Woocher

Editor
Zachary I. Heller

The Susan & David Wilstein Institute of Jewish Policy Studies

Boston and Los Angeles

The publication of this volume has been supported by generous assistance of The Minneapolis Jewish Federation and the Combined Jewish Philanthropies of Greater Boston.

ISBN 1-893380-01-7

Printed in the United States of America

Table of Contents

Contributors

Allan Finkelstein, President of the Jewish Community Centers Association of North America, current Chair of the Professional Advisory Committee for the Hornstein Program at Brandeis University.

David M. Gordis, Director of the Wilstein Institute of Jewish Policy Studies, President and Professor of Rabbinics, Hebrew College.

Zachary I. Heller, Associate Director, Wilstein Institute of Jewish Policy Studies.

Hayim Herring, Assistant Executive Director of the Minneapolis Jewish Federation.

Neuman F. Pollack, Consultant in Organizational Development and Lecturer in Mangement, College of Business, Florida Atlantic University.

Barry Shrage, President, Combined Jewish Philanthropies, Greater Boston.

Alan Silverstein, Rabbi of Congregation Agudath Israel in Caldwell, NJ, President of World Council of Conservative/Masorti Synagogues.

Jonathan S. Woocher, President of the Jewish Educational Service of North America, (JESNA), and chief professional for Jewish Renaissance and Renewal for the United Jewish Communities.

Christopher Winship, Professor of Sociology, Harvard University.

Editor's Preface

Zachary I. Heller

Images and models of a community reflect not only abstract perceptions but may also influence policy formulation. Strategies and modes of action are also the products of such value-laden perceptions. In the lead paper of this volume, *Network Judaism: A New Image for Understanding the Organization of American Jews*, Dr. Hayim Herring poses several significant questions concerning varying views of the Jewish community and how it should function in an age so heavily influenced by new technologies. Herring posits that contemporary challenges to older norms must be accepted as new opportunities. An organizational system based upon a hierarchical model must be replaced by a broader model encompassing a wider range of diverse voices. He has adapted the term "Networking" from the contemporary world of business and technology and proposes that his "network model allows for the flexibility of multiple expressions of Jewishness and Judaism." Barry Shrage's stimulating paper is presented next not in opposition to it, but as a counterpoint to it, viewing the organizing principles of the Jewish community from a different perspective and proposing a framework of new strategies for enhancing its connections and relationships.

Dr. Herring's paper was first presented at a colloquium co-sponsored by the Wilstein Institute of Jewish Policy Studies and JESNA (Jewish Educational Services of North America) in New York City in September 2000. That first reading stimulated a vigorous discussion both among the panelists who were invited to respond to it as well as the select group of participants. The discussion was divided into two segments; the first, focused on the paper as a theoretical construct, the second examined its practical implications. The first panel of respondents included Professor Christopher Winship, Dr. David M. Gordis, and Dr. Jonathan Woocher. The second included Barry Shrage, Rabbi Alan Silverstein and Dr. Allan Finkelstein. Their perceptive and far reaching comments have been summarized and are presented in this volume.

On March 1, 2001 the Wilstein Institute revisited Hayim Herring's paper within the context of its annual academic seminar and public forum at Florida Atlantic University hosted by Dr. Alan L. Berger, Raddock Eminent Scholar Chair and Director of the Program of Holocaust and Judaic Studies at FAU. On that occasion Dr. Herring presented his revised paper and Rabbi Silverstein was the first respondent as a bridge between the original colloquium in New York and this second discussion. Also participating as discussants were Dr. Berger, Mrs. Helen Cohan, Dr. David Gordis, Dr. Neuman Pollock, Rabbi David Steinhardt and Dr. Leon Weissberg. We are grateful to each of them for their contribution of critical insights to those discussions that stimulated Dr. Herring to further revisions of his text. As we began to prepare this volume for the press we decided to include Dr. Neuman Pollock's response along with those from the original colloquium since it added a new perspective to the discussion.

During this process, Barry Shrage revisited his original response and expanded his comments to a fuller statement that the Wilstein Institute feels is a significant counterpoint to Hayim Herring's lead paper. We therefore present them in that sequence followed by the other comments and critiques. The purpose of disseminating this publication is not to provide formulae but to stimulate discussion. As an institute devoted to the analysis of Jewish public policy issues, we hope that these essays and commentaries will cause the reader to pause and re-examine long held perceptions regarding Jewish community, identity and leadership. In the spirit of much of Jewish investigation, the search for good answers must be preceded by the search for significant questions. We hope that this publication will provide some of each.

The Wilstein Institute expresses its deep appreciation to those who participated in the discussions, to the invitees to each of the events who questioned them perceptively, to Dr. Jonathan Woocher, the President of JESNA, who first brought Dr. Herring's work to our attention and co-chaired the original colloquium in New York with Dr. David Gordis, Director of the Wilstein Institute; to Dr. John Ruskay, President of New York UJA-Federation who provided a venue for it; and to Dr. Alan L. Berger of Florida Atlantic University and his staff who provided their usual gracious hospitality for the third in the series of annual Wilstein Institute seminars and forums at FAU.

My personal gratitude to my colleague, Dr. David M. Gordis, who helped shape the original discussions and the format of this publication, and provided his own critical insights in his essay that reflects on the implications of both Hayim Herring's and Barry Shrage's papers

Our Program Associate at the Wilstein Institute's East Coast Center at Hebrew College, James Bornstein, has been very helpful in preparations for the two seminars on which this text is based as well as in its editing.

Network Judaism:
A Fresh Look at the Organization of the American Jewish Community

Rabbi Hayim Herring, Ph.D.

Introduction

For the last twenty-five years, much of the institutional leadership of the American Jewish community has been influenced by a model of community originated by Daniel Elazar, of blessed memory, one of the pre-eminent sociologists of the Jewish community. His model viewed the American Jewish community, ". . . as a series of uneven concentric circles, radiating outward from a hard core of committed Jews toward areas of vague Jewishness on the fringes" *(Community and Polity*, 1995, p.91). The underlying metaphor of this model was a magnet. Elazar viewed the organized Jewish community as a magnet that is able to attract Jews closer to the center based on the degree of their inner Jewish content (that is, the degree of their "iron").

This paper suggests an alternative metaphor for understanding the organization of the American Jewish community. Drawing upon contemporary organizational theory, I recommend that we view the Jewish community as a network organization, that achieves its focused mission through dynamic relationships and not through hierarchical structures. I try to illustrate how this metaphor might help to engage more Jewish individuals more deeply in the life of the Jewish community by giving institutional leadership a new organizational framework for developing policies and programs.

At the outset, I wish to state several of my biases that stimulated the writing of this paper. First, I have worked in and with Jewish institutions for over fifteen years, and I believe in their potential to transform Jews. Almost all of the professionals that I know working within these institutions have a sense of mission that initially called them to their work. However, I also know that much of what we do in institutions is irrelevant for a large segment of the American Jewish community. That knowledge is very painful.

My hope in writing this paper is to encourage institutions to think about how best to present a compelling Jewish vision to contemporary Jews. By doing so, they may be better able to reach individual Jews and their families, who often fail to find a connection to the organized Jewish community. I apologize if some parts of this paper may seem critical to those who work in synagogues and Jewish agencies, however, I hope that such feelings may be mitigated by my strong belief in the value of Jewish organizations and the dedication of the people who work within them.

I have also learned that some people become unsettled when business concepts are applied to the sacred enterprise that we call the Jewish community. They claim that we should not use business and marketing concepts as references, as we are in the "business" of creating communities of meaning and not selling services. While it is certainly an important point to bear in mind, I respectfully disagree with those who take this position. If our central task is to present the depth and breadth of the Jewish civilization, then applying proven business concepts can help us further those objectives. It is precisely because I believe that we have so much to offer, yet we reach relatively so few people, that I endorse the use of business strategies as a tool to promote meaning. Moreover, for better and for worse, business models have invaded most arenas of life. Many doctors, attorneys, non-profit managers, religious leaders and academics will describe the infiltration of business language into their professions. I would rather adapt to this reality than ignore it because I believe that we can be more effective in our work by utilizing some of these concepts.

Metaphor and Management in Organizations

We see the world through the filters of our knowledge and experience. For example, a young IBM manager attended a lecture on paradigms by management expert Joel Arthur Barker. The man was an avid scuba diver, accustomed to diving close to the ocean floor (to the depths of 100–150 feet). Often, at the 150 foot level, he would see Budweiser beer cans with their well-known red label. However, the physics of light only allows green and a few other colors toward the end of the ultraviolet spectrum, but not red, to penetrate through 150 feet of water. How could he see the "red" label? After hearing the talk on paradigms, he realized that because he knew the "correct model" of the beer can, he literally colored the can red in his mind (Barker, 1993, pp.100–101).

This story illustrates a basic truth about how we view the world. We do not observe the world objectively, rather, we look at the world subjectively. Psychologists and sociologists explain that we view the world through individualized filters of experience, knowledge and socialization (Gergen, 1991, pp.81–110). Scientists and philosophers claim that it is our mental paradigms that influence how we see reality (Kuhn, 1996).

In the world of organization and management, Morgan (1999) argues that images or metaphors serve as filters for management theory and behavior. "It [metaphor] is a primal force through which humans create meaning by using one element of experience to understand another" (Morgan, p.4). A range of metaphors currently operates in the world of organizations, from Newtonian mechanistic views (for example, the organization as a machine) to nonlinear organismic views (for example, the organization as a complex adaptive system). Understanding metaphor as a filter for viewing organizations has very significant consequences. As Morgan observes, "Think 'structure' and you'll see structure. Think 'culture' and you'll see all kinds of cultural dimensions. Think 'politics' and you'll find politics. Think in terms of system patterns and loops and you'll find a whole range of them" (Morgan, p.8). Even when organizational metaphors may not be consciously articulated, they produce action strategies. Therefore, Morgan argues that it is critical for organizations to be aware of the metaphors that guide their thinking, as they have practical implications for how they are led and managed.

The Magnet Metaphor: A Dominant Metaphor in Jewish Organizational Life

The American Jewish community is not an organization in the way that a corporation is, rather, it is a community based upon voluntary commitment (Elazar, 1995, p.1). Although the American Jewish community is voluntary in nature, metaphors still function as they do in corporate settings. They inform the expenditure of resources and the development of programs and policies by Jewish organizations. They reflect how American Jewish leadership has responded to the challenges of remaining Jewish in contemporary America.

Is there a dominant metaphor lurking behind the analyses of contemporary American Jewish life? Further study would be required to answer this question definitively. However, it appears that there is one metaphor that seems to serve as a much-used filter for viewing American Jewish life. That metaphor was coined by the late Daniel Elazar, a preeminent sociologist of both the American Jewish community and the global Jewish community. In 1976, Elazar described the American Jewish community, ". . . as a series of uneven concentric circles, radiating outward from a hard core of committed Jews toward areas of vague Jewishness on the fringes" (1995, p.91). Those who inhabit this core, whom Elazar labeled as "integrals," can be defined as Jews, ". . . whose Jewishness is a full-time concern, the central factor of their lives, whether expressed in traditionally religious terms (the vast majority of integral Jews in the U.S.) or through some variety of ethnic nationalism or an intensive involvement in Jewish affairs" (Elazar, p.95).

Elazar then drew six concentric circles around the core, labeling Jews in each ring differently: participants, affiliated Jews, contributors and consumers, peripherals, repudiators and converts out, and quasi-Jews. One can argue with the accuracy of both the number of circles and the way that Elazar categorized Jews in each ring, however, his point was that the core represents the most engaged part of the Jewish population. The further one moves from the core, the less involved the individual. Moreover, according to Elazar, it is the core that serves to attract those in the other circles ever-closer inward.

What is the image, then, behind this notion of a core and a periphery? Elazar explicitly provides an answer.

> Perhaps the most appropriate image for this is a magnet, able to attract iron particles that come within its magnetic field. This is the condition of American Jewry and, increasingly, all of Diaspora Jewry: a magnet at the core pulls those who contain within them the iron filings of Judaism closer to the center, more or less according to the degree of their iron (i.e., Jewish) content (Elazar, 1995, p.100).

In more recent writings, Elazar again drew upon that image, describing the American Jewish community as, ". . . held together by the strength and magnetism of its core, rather than by clear boundaries at its peripheries . . ." (Elazar, 1995, p.1).

According to Elazar, it is the core that shapes organized Jewish life in America. "The magnetism of the core makes its real impact felt through the institutions of the community . . ." (Elazar, 1995, p.2). Elazar seems to imply that the institutions of the Jewish community are the instrumentality through which the core asserts its magnetic pull on individual Jews who are outside of it.

As stated previously, a more thorough analysis would be required to determine if this image of the Jewish community (i.e., the institutions) as a magnet that attracts the iron particles (i.e., individual Jews) is the dominant organizational metaphor. Yet, even without such a study, a case can be made that it is prevalent and influential, even if it is not the exclusive one.

This claim is made on the basis of several observations. First, it is interesting to note that the 1990 National Jewish Population Survey (NJPS) spoke of a segment of Jews that comprised the "core Jewish population" (Kosmin, B., Goldstein, S., Waksberg, J., Lerer, N., Keysar, A. and Scheckner, J.). While precise records do not exist, some 15,000–25,000 copies of the summary findings of this document were distributed to the professional and volunteer leadership of the organized Jewish community (Kosmin, personal interview with the author, August 25, 1997). With regard to publications that reach the professional and volunteer leadership of this audience, this is certainly a very large number.

The research staff of the United Jewish Communities estimates that at least 150 magazine and newspaper articles were written about the 1990 NJPS. While not all of them referred to a "core" Jewish population, many of them did. This unprecedented media coverage was likely to further promote the image of a core Jewish population. Naturally, a "core" implies some kind of "periphery" that is secondary in some way to the "core."

In November 1993, the North American Commission on Jewish Identity and Continuity was assembled to provide a response to the 1990

NJPS that would stimulate Jewish continuity. Another clue to the prominence of the magnet metaphor may be found in this Commission's final report, *The Report of the North American Commission on Jewish Identity and Continuity*. Like the 1990 NJPS, this report was also heavily distributed throughout the organized Jewish community. This report also speaks about engaging "target populations," that is, those who are the targets of the core's efforts. One of the Commission's four objectives was, "Engaging diverse populations: (developing) strategies for reaching and involving Jews outside the intensely affiliated core" (Report on the North American Commission on Jewish Identity and Continuity, 1995, p. ix). In other words, consciously or unconsciously, this report also seems to have drawn upon the metaphor of a magnetic core for framing its understanding of the condition of American Judaism.

Several years ago, twenty-two leading Jewish theologians, academics and directors of organizations from a diverse spectrum of Jewish life issued a "Statement of Jewish Continuity." In that document, they again alluded to the image of the organized Jewish community as a magnet for "peripheral" Jews.

> In recent years, Jewish leaders have initiated programs of outreach-to-Jews in an effort to draw Jews closer to their people and faith and to win back those whose Judaism has eroded. The moderately affiliated are the most promising candidates for kiruv (outreach), and given scarce resources outreach programs are most productively directed toward them. . . . But these efforts must not be allowed to siphon away funds urgently needed to strengthen Jewish life at its core (Statement on Jewish Continuity, n.d.).

One last example will suffice to support the assertion of the centrality of the magnet image. Three leading researchers of the American Jewish community published an article entitled, "How to Save American Jews" (Wertheimer, Liebman and Cohen, 1996). The substance of their article, more of which will be discussed later, is that the Jewish community would do best to invest its limited resources in the core population so that it can serve to attract those on the periphery.

For Jews on the margins who may be surfeited with
rootlessness and looking for something authentic in
their lives, the existence of an enthusiastic and fulfilled
core population, a population offering a genuine alternative, can surely act as a more powerful lure than the
bland nostrums of an establishment that offers, in
effect, only another version of what already ails them.
Such a core population exists—and with careful nurturing it can become even more highly engaged and
much more numerous than it already is (Wertheimer et
al, p.51).

From these several examples, it appears that the metaphor of a magnetic institutional core attracting individual Jews underlies the way that
a diverse array of Jewish leadership views the organized Jewish community. The selections quoted represent different disciplines and religious
denominations within the applied and academic leadership of the Jewish
community. While other images may inform the thinking about the
organized Jewish community, this author is not aware of any other that is
so dominant.

It is not evident that Elazar meant his descriptive metaphor to serve
as the basis for Jewish policy makers to develop and implement policies.
Indeed, Elazar frequently questioned how representative Jewish institutional leadership was of the American Jewish community (Bubis, 2000;
Elazar, 1997, pp.14–18; Elazar, 1995, pp.391–393). "Even when there is
one voice speaking on behalf of organized Jewry, it represents only a small
part of those concerned" (Elazar and Gerstenfeld, 1999).

While Elazar did not advocate that the Jewish institutional "elite" be
empowered to make decisions for the broader "Jewish republic," that
appears to have happened in many cases. Elazar's description of the Jewish
community has become a frequent prescription for Jewish leaders who
wish to direct the resources of their institutions to the "core" and away
from the "periphery." This reality confirms Morgan's contention that
metaphors have consequences, so we do need to be aware of the metaphors
that shape our organizations.

Memes and the Magnet Metaphor

How is it that one image could become so prevalent among such a diverse group of thinkers and leaders? The relatively new field of memetics may offer a framework for understanding this phenomenon. Richard Dawkins, who first coined the term memes in 1976, explains that,

> Examples of memes are tunes, ideas, catch-phrases, clothes fashions, ways of making pots or building arches. Just as genes propagate themselves in the gene pool by leaping from body to body via sperm or eggs, so memes propagate themselves in the meme pool by leaping from brain to brain via a process, which, in the broad sense, can be called imitation. If a scientist hears, or reads about, a good idea, he passes it on to his colleagues and students. He mentions it in his articles and lectures. If the idea catches on, it can be said to propagate itself, spreading from brain to brain (Dawkins, 2000).

In other words, a meme can be thought of as a "virus of the mind" (Brodie, 1996). Like viruses, memes are intent on replicating themselves. Moreover, a meme's ability to replicate itself does not depend upon whether or not it is true. From the many previous examples of the magnet metaphor, it appears that it is a successful meme that has propagated itself in the minds of a diverse group of thinkers, policy makers, academicians and practitioners.

Five Limitations of the Magnet Metaphor

Despite its prevalence, the magnet metaphor is very limiting and no longer very helpful for shaping policies and programs for the American Jewish community. It is unhelpful because:

1. it only views the structure of the Jewish community through an institutional lens and does not draw upon more recent organizational theory,

2. it is a metaphor that polarizes discussion around different segments of the Jewish community,

3. it ignores patterns of geographic mobility in the American Jewish community,

4. it does not address generational differences of involvement in the Jewish community,

5. it ignores the broader context in which contemporary Jews live today.

Each of these limitations will be explored below in greater detail.

The Magnet Metaphor: Only One Possible Lens

As Morgan observes, the paradox of any metaphor is that it both expands and restricts understanding. It expands understanding by enabling the application of insights from other areas of experience, however, it limits understanding by analyzing an issue through a single perspective (Morgan, p.9). One of the limitations of this metaphor is that it views Jewish life through an institutional perspective organized in a hierarchical manner. While that is a valid framework, it is not the only possible one. Moreover, it is a perspective that does not incorporate a more recent understanding of contemporary organizational dynamics.

Consider this: the majority of Jews in America do not pay dues to a synagogue, the premiere institution of Jewish life (Kosmin et al, 1990). Nor do the vast majority of American Jews practice some central Jewish rituals, like prayer and Sabbath observance. Therefore, from an institutional perspective, they are not a part of the "core" Jewish population. Nevertheless, individual Jews who do not meet the criteria of institutional involvement may actually lead rich Jewish lives. Sales and Tobin, (p.8, 1995), writing on church and synagogue affiliation, note that, ". . . affiliation is not tantamount to religiosity. An individual may be intensely religious, hold deep spiritual beliefs, and be well educated in a religious tradition but not be a member of a congregation." Yet, do such Jews who do not belong to a synagogue ascribe the categories of "core" and "peripheral" to their own Jewish lives? Indeed, have we asked what metaphors individuals might use when describing the Jewish community? Core and periphery are not very meaningful categories when viewed through a more grassroots, individual perspective.

Whether the Jewish community is viewed through an institutional lens or, for example, through an individual lens, has significant implications. If framed from an institutional perspective, the issue becomes how to get more individual Jews involved in Jewish institutions. Accordingly, resources are invested in ways to better market the services of an institution or to make it more attractive. But, the questions are very different if framed from an individual perspective. Individuals may raise issues like the need to belong to so many different organizations to receive services, and question the quality, accessibility and effectiveness of those services. These questions imply a need for a greater investment of institutional resources into individual Jews and their families. Therefore, both institutions and individuals are likely to feel frustrated over policy and program strategies because each is asking a different and sometimes contradictory set of questions based on the way that they look at the Jewish community.

Another serious limitation of this metaphor is that it does not draw upon more recent literature about how people organize themselves in contemporary society. The magnet model is based on a traditional, linear, "command and control" centralized model of organization. In traditional organizational models, the assumption is that a small group of people at the top can set goals and objectives for others at the bottom. It is the equivalent of the "father knows best" model of parenting for organizations, where all of the wisdom is centralized in one person (or, in the case of organizations, in one office). The job of the people at the bottom is to carry out the plan devised by the people at the top.

By analogy, in the magnet metaphor, the people in the core are like the people at the top of the organizational pyramid, and those on the periphery are like those at the bottom. This metaphor is based on the view that the people at the top know what is best for those below them. The job of those inside the core is to plan in such a way as to bring more people closer to the core. Thus, their activities are directed at them, often without sufficient knowledge of what those on the periphery actually need or want.

This classical view of organization is based on a Newtonian view of the world (Eoyang, 1997; Morgan, 1998; Petzinger, 1999), however, the principles of a Newtonian world-view are under attack. Therefore, it is reasonable to question the management models that derive from this world-view (Merry, 1999). Just as in the physical realm there is a recognition that the world consists of open, interdependent systems, in the world of organizations, there is an increasing recognition that organizations are really open, dynamic interdependent systems. The magnet metaphor does not fully capture the open, dynamic nature of Jewish community today.

The Magnet Metaphor Is Polarizing and Judgmental

Another problem with the magnet metaphor is that it is inherently polarizing. By structuring the American Jewish community around a core and periphery, it suggests that people on the periphery are somehow a problem. Depending upon one's perspective, they are either "at risk," "disloyal," or "target populations" in need of intervention from the organized Jewish community. The magnet metaphor invites moral judgments about Jewish life that are often destructive by labeling Jews in the "core" as good Jews, and those outside as bad Jews.

The value of the magnet metaphor is that it encourages deliberation about resource allocation, but the by-product of this metaphor is often intense debates about the amount of resources that should be allocated to those on the periphery. From an institutional perspective, questions are raised about how much effort to put into the core, which has already demonstrated a certain level of commitment to the organized community, as opposed to how valuable it is to try to re-attract those who have drifted out of the core's magnetic pull.

For example, as noted previously, some argue that it is better to strengthen the core so that it can continue to have a magnetic effect. However, no research has ever been conducted to test the hypothesis that an intensified core will have a stronger magnetic pull. Perhaps investing resources into the core population only produces a more intensive core. Alternatively, others argue that the way to increase the core is to reach out actively to those on the periphery and develop programs and services that will bring them closer to the core.

Regardless of the position that one takes on this issue, the point remains the same. The magnet metaphor encourages a polarized and judgmental debate about resource allocation to those in the "core" as opposed to those on the "periphery." It does not invite leadership to think in a "both/and" mode. If a high-quality program is marketed sensitively, it may very well be able to encompass both so-called "core" Jews and "peripheral" Jews.

The Magnet Metaphor Misses Patterns of Geographic Mobility

The magnet metaphor also ignores the great geographic mobility of American Jews (Kosmin et al, 1990). Often, American Jews cannot become involved in Jewish organizations because they are no longer living near them. Or, they decide not to join an organization because they are unsure of when their next move may be. Sometimes, institutional policies around involvement in an organization assume a permanent, stable, physical address for individuals who may not be thinking in those terms. In actuality, the more stable address for the moment might be a person's email address in cyberspace, a place that Jewish organizations are just learning to exploit.

The Magnet Metaphor Does Not Address Generational Differences in Involvement

This metaphor also ignores a relatively new phenomenon in contemporary America. Thanks to advances in health and medical science, we are experiencing the reality of having significant numbers of four generations of people living and working at the same time for the first time in history. Zemke, Raines and Filipczak (2000) provide a useful typology of each generation: "Veterans" are those individuals shaped by the Depression, World War II and the Korean War; "Boomers" are those for whom the Kennedy assassination, the Vietnam War and the Women's Liberation Movement were formative events; "Gen X'ers" are those shaped by cultural phenomena like MTV, single-parent families, AIDS and computers; and, "Nexters," the emerging generation, is being influenced by a more pervasive existence of technology that is enabling them to grow up in a truly global village.

Research has shown that the different characteristics of these four generations affect their attitudes toward organizations. For example, while "veterans" tend to be more loyal to organizations (Zemke et al, pp.36–42), "Gen X'ers," having watched their boomer parents "downsized," tend to be very skeptical about allegiance to organizations (Zemke et al, pp.97–102). The magnet metaphor takes a blunt look at American Jews, and does not evaluate their patterns of participation in organizational life according to these more subtle demographic profiles. As the existence of multiple generations of Jews will be a permanent feature of life, it will be important to develop metaphors that are more sensitive to these differences.

The Magnet Metaphor Does Not Fully Address Life Beyond the Periphery

During the initial writing of this paper, Senator Joseph Lieberman was a candidate for Vice-President of the United States of America while at the same time, some non-Jewish pop culture stars (like Madonna) were studying Kabbalah. Clearly, no one anticipated such developments in 1976 when the magnet metaphor first appeared. These two examples illustrate that Jewish life and culture is mainstream today. That is no surprise because most Jews spend more time outside of the Jewish community than inside of it. The magnet metaphor does not take a broader systems approach to Jewish community; it implies that there is an abyss beyond the last ring of the periphery that has no impact on what happens within the different rings. It does not take into account that most Jews live within the mainstream of American culture and are influenced by it.

An Urgent Need for Change

Even in his later writings, Elazar still seems to have used the magnet metaphor as an analytical tool for understanding the organized Jewish community. Yet, he still fully grasped the privatized, individualized, and customized nature of Jewish life in America.

> The American Jewish community, the first fully emancipated Jewish community, is entirely a product of the modern epoch. As such, it is in most respects a model of what Jewish life has become or is becoming for all but a handful of Jews in the world: based on the voluntary commitment, through a variety of paths of those

individuals who care to be Jewish, few of whom feel
obligated or compelled (1995, p.1).

He added, "Moreover, since the community is a voluntary one, per-
suasion rather than compulsion, influence rather than power, are the tools
available for making decisions and implementing policies" (Elazar, 1995,
p.3). Unfortunately, Elazar did not try to conceptualize a model of
American Jewish life that accounted for the customized and personalized
inclinations of individual Jews in contemporary America.

It is also important to note that American Jews are not the only ones
to customize their ethnic or religious identity. As noted by Waters
(1990), ethnicity in America is optional. While it seems strange that ethnicity should be anything but inherited, Waters found that for Americans
of white, European ancestry, ethnicity is a matter of personal preference
and not inheritance. Thus, the issue of the obligatory nature of Jewish life
is not just a Jewish issue.

As Israel (1999) notes:

To be blunt, if the Italians or Irish or Scots were Jews,
they would be wailing about Italian or Irish or Scottish
continuity. The weakening of communal ties, in the
form of group distinctiveness, is not just a Jewish phenomenon.

Recognizing that automatic loyalty to organizational life is an issue
for many ethnic groups suggests that Jewish organizations cannot expect
significant numbers of individual Jews to adhere to predetermined communal norms. Indeed, Israel estimates that only 25% of the American
Jews can be considered core Jews today. Thus, the magnet metaphor that
reflects an institutional perspective does not account for the vast majority of American Jews today.

Increasingly, some Jewish researchers and leaders are invoking the
need for institutional change (Israel, 1999; Cohen and Eisen, 1998) as the
solution to engaging more Jews in the lives of Jewish institutions.
Jonathan Woocher (1999) forcefully summarizes these sentiments for
change.

Like other Americans, Jews today are often suspicious of all institutions. They react warily at best, with hostility at worst, to a priori 'demands' and 'expectations.' They have not abandoned the quest for community belonging—indeed, they often bemoan its absence in their lives. But they are seeking to experience connection in ways that are more intimate and personal than most institutions appear to offer, and without giving up their autonomy. They want responsive institutions, which neither take for granted their loyalty and involvement, nor leave them feeling empty and unnoticed as they participate. They are willing to give of themselves—at least up to a point—but they do want to receive something valuable in return, for themselves and for their families.

It does appear that institutional change efforts are becoming more common among Jewish institutions. Synagogue 2000 is one such project that is promoting organizational change within Reform and Conservative synagogues. The Jewish Community Centers Association and the Hillel Foundation for Jewish Life on Campus have undergone significant change processes. Of course, the recent merger of the Council of Jewish Federations, the United Israel Appeal and the United Jewish Appeal into the United Jewish Communities reflects another major institutional change process at work that is designed to make a system both more efficient and more responsive.

The Limitations of Current Institutional Change Efforts

Clearly, these calls for institutional change are welcome. They may, over time, produce greater participation in the life of the organized Jewish community, however, my hunch is that they will not likely succeed in the dramatic ways envisioned by those who champion these efforts. The reason for this hunch is that these "change efforts" are still predicated on the magnet model of institutional life. They still frame issues of individual involvement from an institutional perspective, albeit a perspective that is much more customer-oriented. They still presume that Jews should willingly be part of some command and control central.

They still place the people involved in institutional life at the top of the organizational pyramid, while ignoring the vast majority of American Jews who have sporadic or no institutional affiliation. They ignore the fact that people today are typically not interested in having anyone or anything tell them how to live their lives or set goals for them.

As it is often the corporate world that has inspired these reengineering efforts, it is no surprise that they share some of the same weaknesses as corporate reengineering. One corporate expert explains, "The danger in re-engineering, however, is that it merely reinforces the top-down, hierarchical, organizational model of the past century while masquerading as a revolutionary change" (Dent, 1998, p.136). Reengineering may only amount to tinkering with a model that is still hierarchical. People at the top (although fewer in number) still serve as the command and control center for the people at the bottom (also fewer in number). Dent notes that no matter how re-engineered a company is, as long as it is organized along the lines of a traditional, hierarchical model, it will not be able to respond quickly enough to consumer needs (Dent, p.136). That will be true of reengineering efforts in the Jewish community.

A New Frontier

In order to develop a new metaphor for understanding the organization of American Jews today, it is important to examine some of the broader changes that have occurred in the past decade in contemporary America, especially in the corporate sector. Petzinger (1999, pp.21–25) summarizes some of the major changes of the 1990's. He notes that as painful as the downsizing of the 1990's was, it unleashed a business revolution. For example, for every job eliminated in the mid-1990's, 1.5 jobs were created primarily in small firms, and that is significant because small firms innovate at twice the rate of large ones.

Demographic changes also propelled this business revolution. Boomers, who came into power during this time, began to "question authority" and were open to new ways of doing business. They introduced the notion of finding "meaning" on a personal level at work. Women, who entered management level positions in significant numbers at this time, helped to fuel discussions about the dignity of each individual in the corporate workplace.

Finally, intellectual and technological change fueled a change in the business world. Systems thinking began to penetrate the business world, challenging workers to understand the interconnected nature of "components" of work that had been seen as separate. Personal desktop computing and the creation of a global infrastructure through the Internet reinforced and created that interconnected universe.

Changes in technology are so pervasive that they have radically changed the business environments in which people work, and the expectations of most individuals in contemporary society (Gates, 1999, pp.xv–xvi). Individuals can be matched with one another based on common interests in a way not possible before. The Internet is a universal space for information sharing, collaboration, and commerce that encompasses numbers, text, sound and video. We will soon live in a world in which we will be online all of the time (Friedman, 2000, p.201). All electronic devices, from refrigerators to hand-held personal communications tools, are being fitted with software that connects to the Internet through homes, offices, and satellites. In fact, its reach is becoming so pervasive, that Friedman has dubbed it the Evernet (p.201).

Clearly, the 1990's helped to launch a new business era. Petzinger (p.17) refers to it as a "new frontier" for human existence.

> It is a frontier of technologies, ideas and values. The
> pioneers celebrate individuality over conformity among
> their employees and customers alike. They deploy tech-
> nology to distribute rather than consolidate authority
> and creativity. They compete through resilience instead
> of resistance, through adaptation instead of control. In
> a time of dizzying complexity and change, they realize
> that tightly drawn strategies become brittle while
> shared purpose endures.

If business is defining the new frontier, then it is from business that we might search for a new metaphor that can help guide a reorganization of the Jewish community in America.

Network Judaism: A New Way
of Understanding Community

Where is the real business revolution that has serious implications for the Jewish community? It is in network organizations (Gates, 2000; Dent, 1998; Lipnack and Stamps, 1994). "The network is emerging as the signature form of organization in the Information Age, just as bureaucracy stamped the Industrial Age, hierarchy controlled the Agricultural Era, and the small group roamed the Nomadic Era" (Lipnack and Stamps, p.3). "We predict that they (network organizations) are the future institution. We anticipate . . . that this new institutional form will increasingly replace both markets and hierarchies as a governance mechanism" (Alter and Hage, 1993, p.13).

The word network may evoke a picture of a computer network. However, network organizations are not merely organizations that use technology extensively and wisely, rather, the word network describes a set of internal and external organizational relationships. Unlike organizations that are arranged hierarchically, "The word 'network' evokes a clear, simple mental model, a structure of points or circles and connecting lines —nodes and links, vibrant with activity" (Lipnack and Stamps, p.86). Others define a network organization as, ". . . any collection of actors (N > 2) that pursue repeated, enduring exchange relations with one another and, at the same time, lack a legitimate organizational authority to arbitrate and resolve disputes that may arise during the exchange" (Polodny and Page, 1998). Powell stresses the characteristic of mutual interest as opposed to self-interest in network organizations. "In essence, the parties to a network agree to forego the right to pursue their own interests at the expense of others" (p.303). Dent (p.137) writes that, "The network organization consists of leaders, guiding entrepreneurs, and self-managing teams in a chaotic, real-time process that is organized around the ever-changing needs of individual customers."

I would like to offer my definition of network organizations: at least two organizations that, while retaining their autonomy and identity, agree to work together to provide a higher level of service to an identified constituency than they can provide individually. Participants in a network share jointly in the burdens and benefits of working together.

In the scholarly and business literature on organizations, no single definition of a network organization has gained universal acceptance, yet, some common themes about network organizations emerge from this literature. For the purposes of this paper, in identifying these themes, I have drawn upon Dent (1998), Gates (1999), Lipnack and Stamps (1994), Polody and Page (1998), and Powell (1990).

Network organizations are characterized by a high degree of real-time communications, both within an organization and among the members of a network. This high degree of communications enables network organizations to react in a timely fashion to changes in the environment. These communications cannot be enforced but are voluntary in nature.

Network organizations are also noted for their clarity of purpose or vision. Members of a network organization have different but complementary specialties so each member retains its independence. Network organizations are also characterized by a high degree of collaboration, and form teams around specific projects. This is true both within organizations and across organizations. Leadership is therefore not pre-assigned by rank, but determined according to the task at hand.

In network organizations, technology is a means to an end. Network organizations use technology in order to organize people in ways that greatly enhances their responsiveness to those within and outside of their organization. Technology is used to organize people so that they can relate more directly and personally to one another.

Leadership is at the center of the network organization. It establishes the focus of the organization, the organizational culture and rules for decision-making within an organization. The role of leadership is to diffuse decision-making. Leadership allows teams to make decisions, especially those at the front lines, and to be responsive to customer needs. Thus, leadership creates a culture of feedback and responsiveness among members of the network organization, and between individual organizations and customers. Clearly, leadership in this model is less exclusive than in traditional, hierarchical organizations.

In summary, network organizations are better suited to contemporary life.

> Our central argument is that systemic networks—clusters of organizations that make decisions jointly and integrate their efforts to produce a product or service—adjust more rapidly to changing technologies and market conditions, develop new products and services in a shorter time period, and provide more creative solutions in the process (Alter and Hage, p.2).

When organizations are wired in network relationships they have the ability to provide higher quality products at a faster rate.

Illustrating the Network Judaism Model

Rather than talk theory, let us take an imaginary tour of what a networked Jewish community might look like from the perspective of the individual. We will name this individual Ben Bayit, and follow him through this networked community as he seeks to have his Jewish needs addressed. Ben is married to Beth, who is not Jewish, and they have two children (Burt and Belinda) who are in the primary grades, one of whom has a learning disability. They have just moved to a new community, and decided that they would like certain services.

Ben calls the Jewish Community "hot line for help" number, but the line is busy. He then logs on to the Jewish Community web site, and identifies several synagogues near his home. However, the nearest synagogue is 20 miles from his home and he does not want to have to rely solely upon his SUV to get him to one, given the harsh weather he sometimes experiences. Fortunately, one synagogue televises its religious services, that he can watch either on his computer or on his local cable television channel. In fact, he can even participate in services and study groups electronically. Educational materials for classes are posted each week on the synagogue's web site, and real-time discussion groups are available several times each week.

Ben scans the kinds of different religious services that are offered, but none of the four different *minyanim* at the nearest synagogue are to his liking. He contacts the Prayer Innovation Director (PID), and outlines his ideas about the kind of service he is interested in experiencing. The PID queries the entire synagogue membership about their interest in this kind of service, and receives 25 positive responses. The PID then emails Ben that in 4 weeks, the kind of service that he was seeking will be available. Ben and the PID then set a time to meet and work out the details, as they will coordinate the service. This service is advertised both in the synagogue's communication vehicles, and in the general media (print, television, radio and electronic). Especially important to Ben is that the service have an interpreter for the hearing impaired.

Ben is willing to try this synagogue to see if it meets the spiritual needs of his family. He then takes out a six-month trial membership that he pays for over the Internet. This trial membership includes several incentive packages. For example, it allows Ben and his family to use the Jewish Community Center and its satellite office that is only five miles from his home. The satellite office includes a media resource center, childcare services and occasional plays and concerts of a Jewish nature. In addition, there are special discount packages for the local art museum, which has partnered with the Jewish Community Center to offer some traveling Jewish exhibits, and the local symphony that features occasional programs of Jewish music. In addition, a special needs coordinator from the Jewish Community Education Services Office will assess the needs of his special needs child.

The next day, Beth receives a call from Wendy, the Welcome Committee member. The committee member expresses her delight in Beth's interest, and offers to meet her either at her home, at the synagogue or wherever it is convenient to learn more about what she and her husband are seeking and how else they might become involved. The following day, the Bayit family receives a letter from the synagogue staff welcoming them, and a video and CD-ROM with family activities. They also receive some materials on all of the institutions in the Jewish community that may be of interest to them. The day after, the rabbi contacts them and encourages them to learn about the congregation and ask questions that they may have about it.

Beth and Ben Bayit decide to have Wendy, the Welcome Committee member, to their home. Beth and Ben are concerned that their family may not feel welcome because Beth is not Jewish, nor does she have interest at this time in converting to Judaism. Wendy reassures Beth and Ben that the role of the synagogue is to give them access to information, experiences and people that will be of use and interest to them; they will decide what to do with these resources. Wendy suggests that they meet with their Jewish family educator, who will customize a family learning plan for them. They can either learn in the synagogue, the Jewish Community Center satellite office, or on their own with periodic visits from the family educator. The Bayit family starts to feel at home in the Jewish community, and they become members of this synagogue and participants in the broader Jewish community.

This fictitious scenario could actually happen if Jewish institutions:

- abandoned their often cumbersome committee structure;

- made it easier, fun and more meaningful to participate in Jewish life;

- had user-friendly policies that were sensitive to individual needs;

- had rapid response-times to inquiries from members;

- had partnerships with other Jewish institutions and other cultural and educational institutions in the broader community; and,

- understood the value of information and marketing and knew how to exploit technology to increase institutional responsiveness to individual needs.

However, synagogues, and other institutions that comprise the organized Jewish community, have generally not learned how to dismantle the institutional barriers that prevent much broader participation in Jewish life.

Overcoming the Limitations of the Magnet Metaphor

As noted previously, there are five limitations to the magnet metaphor:

1. it only views the structure of the Jewish community through an institutional lens,

2. it polarizes discussion around different segments of the Jewish community,

3. it ignores patterns of geographic mobility in the American Jewish community,

4. it does not address generational differences of involvement in the Jewish community,

5. it ignores the broader context in which contemporary Jews live today. From the illustration of the network metaphor using the Bayit family, we gain some insight into how these limitations are overcome.

In the network model, for those who are accustomed to thinking in terms of pyramids, it is the individual and not the organization that is at the top of the pyramid. (Actually, there is no pyramid at all, just interconnected networks.) This metaphor recognizes that individuals access Jewish life on an as-needed basis. Individuals want to connect to community portals on their own terms and they demand responsiveness. If organizations are unresponsive, they go elsewhere, either in real space or cyberspace. They create their own life cycle ceremonies, their own liturgies and publications, and their unique and idiosyncratic ways of being Jewish (Horovitz, 2000).

Elazar's model of Jewish life places Jewish institutions at the heart of community. All institutions are defined by a set of expectations to which individuals are expected to adhere, or at least support. Moreover, as noted previously, there often seems to be a presumption on the part of institutions that the more an individual conforms to a certain set of Jewish behaviors the better that person is in the eyes of institutions.

In contrast to Elazar's conception of community, the network organization model places the individual at the center of community. Therefore, as we see with the Bayit family, the network model allows for the flexibility of multiple expressions of Jewishness and Judaism. As we move into this new era of "postmodernity," characterized by diverse and customized forms of Jewish identity, this change in focus from institutions to individuals becomes increasingly important as it creates greater opportunities for individuals to participate in Jewish life—both within institutions and outside of them.

The network metaphor, as applied to Jewish institutional life, does not eliminate all arguments about the allocation of resources. Clearly, successful organizations learn to focus their resources toward their mission and objectives, however, the network metaphor can help institutions recast the terms of the debate about resource allocation. It does not automatically prejudge whether certain kinds of Jews are more or less central to the Jewish community, but it does ask institutions to evaluate their capacity to build relationships with individuals by being more responsive to their needs.

That does not mean that every expressed need can or should be met. But, this metaphor encourages institutions to put more emphasis on connecting individuals and less on castigating them. In responding to that challenge, the network metaphor may help institutions think about how to provide programs that are more encompassing in their scope, independent of the imposed labels of "core" and "periphery." In the magnet model mindset, the Bayit family might have been deemed unworthy of attention. In contrast, the network model allows both their needs and the needs of other members of their congregation to be simultaneously met.

In the Bayit family illustration, we also view another advantage of the network metaphor. It explicitly acknowledges that Jews, even those with rich institutional lives, live in multiple communities and not just the Jewish community. Network thinking may stimulate institutions to make stronger connections both within the Jewish community and across the Jewish community, to those other places where Jews live much of their daily lives. Thus, the Bayit family is able to purchase a membership package that allows them to participate in their synagogue, the Jewish Community Center, and some cultural events in their general community.

To some extent, the network model also has an inherent capacity to address the geographic mobility of the Jewish community in several ways. First, with its emphasis on institutions networking more with one another, it allows for the possibility of collaborations that have a stronger appeal than any single institution may have on its own. That appeal may be advantageous in attracting newcomers to participate in the life of their new Jewish community.

Moreover, the magnet metaphor may inadvertently label a Jew that had been in the "core" in one community as "peripheral" (and therefore less worthy of attention) in another if that person delays or defers institutional affiliation in a new community. In contrast, the network metaphor avoids that inadvertent trap, and encourages institutions to think more flexibly about policies that are in tune with a mobile population.

The network Judaism model also takes a more subtle look at the different generational attitudes toward institutional membership. It does not presume that Jews and their families will join institutions automatically, at a given stage of life. As we saw with the Bayit family, the network metaphor's emphasis on responsiveness and relationship building may have a greater appeal to "Boomers" and "Gen X'ers."

The Bayit Family: Coming to a Neighborhood Near You

While the tale of the Bayit family is fictional, it is still true because it is an accurate description of emerging Jewish life today, supported by scientifically sound demographic studies and new qualitative research previously noted. Individuals are often constructing their Jewish lives around Jewish institutions instead of through them, because of their perceived lack of responsiveness and prior expectations. "One of the major issues for our community in contemporary America is the increasing gap between the current systems of organized Jewish life and the lives of most 21st-century Jews" (Israel, 2000).

For example, grassroots Judaism is expressing itself in many interesting forms. A business entrepreneur recently purchased a magazine called *Being Jewish*, that had 17,000 subscribers. After its third issue, this entrepreneur had used his skills to boost the number of subscribers to over 95,000. This magazine is not published by any organization, yet now has one of the largest subscription rates of Jewish periodicals in the country. JewishFamily.com has created a virtual Jewish community with a list of over six different sites (like teens and interfaith families) that individuals and families can explore. While no study has been formally conducted, anecdotally, there appears to be a growth of non-denominational synagogues, some with and some without rabbis. These are just a few examples of individual Jews bypassing Jewish institutions when constructing their Jewish identity.

In a computer network, hardware and software have to be compatible. We might think of Jewish institutions as the hardware of the Jewish community, and individuals as the software or operating systems.

Currently, for many, there is a lack of compatibility between the hardware and the operating systems. Therefore, as the above examples suggest, the operating systems are driving the creation of new hardware. While the growth of new organizations is welcome, there is still great potential value in linking up individuals with existing organizations rather than circumventing them.

Pearson (1999), citing the father of modern management, Henri Fayol, suggests that there are five principles of management that are highly relevant to organizations today: (1) planning, (2) organizing, (3) commanding, (4) coordinating and, (5) controlling. However, in today's information age, Pearson suggests that less emphasis should be on controlling, and more placed on planning, organizing, commanding, and coordinating. I would substitute "leading" for "commanding," as commanding has overtones of dominance.

Planning, organizing, leading and coordinating; these are all activities suited to the network Judaism model. These activities are meant to more directly serve the individuals for whom organizations were invented in the first place. They respect the role of the individual in constructing a personalized Jewish life, and direct institutional resources toward that end.

Institutional Implications for Network Judaism

Understanding the Jewish community as a network organization does present some serious issues to Jewish institutions. First, it challenges institutional leadership to think differently about how individuals may relate to Jewish institutions. Almost all of the different religious, social, cultural and educational institutions have core values, principles, theologies or ideologies that function as boundaries, no matter how permeable these boundaries are. Therefore, institutional leadership will have to clearly articulate their core values and boundaries so as not to frustrate potential users and to honor their own integrity. However, within the boundaries of their mission, they can learn to be as responsive as possible. Mission driven, market sensitive; this slogan can help organizations maintain their integrity while still being challenged to better understand and respond to those who seek their services.

The network Judaism model of community also asks institutional leadership to reexamine how institutions function internally. In order to be more responsive to individual needs, a fundamental reorganization and retraining of staff and volunteers along a network model will be necessary. In fact, more staff may be necessary to meet individual needs and to work on collaborative projects. Additionally, a truly networked organization will require a more sophisticated use of technology and marketing strategies.

Network Judaism also asks institutional leadership to examine how Jewish institutions relate to one another. Organizations that exist in a network relationship do not compete against one another, but work together to be responsive to consumers. The kind of orientation that places the needs of the individual ahead of the position of one organization requires real collaboration.

Finally, network Judaism asks institutions to think about how to reach Jews outside of their own institutional spaces. Many creative collaborations—with universities, hospitals, law firms, cultural institutions, and retail stores—can be developed to reach Jews when they are not in Jewish institutions (which is the vast majority of the time). Such partnerships, if consciously and vigorously pursued by institutions, can extend the reach of many Jewish organizations.

Technology: A Means to an End

Clearly, we are living at a time of great social disruption. The changes in the way that individuals relate to organizations of all kinds has been well documented (Fukuyama, 1999; Putnam, 2000), as has a decline in the existence of community as this term has been understood historically. With the increasing use of technology, the desire to create real (as opposed to virtual) community becomes an even greater concern.

However, it is worth remembering what the "P" in "PC" stands for: **personal** computer. Technology is not an end unto itself, or a substitute for real-time communities, rather, it is a tool to create more human and personalized relationships between individuals, and between individuals and communities. As Friedman notes:

> But these much needed values (of community and spir-
> itual meaning) are best learned off-line, outside the
> Internet. The only way people are going to find God
> on the Internet is if they bring Him there in their own
> heads and hearts and behaviors—drawing on values
> they learn in the terrestial world—in the olive groves
> of their parents' home or their community, church,
> synagogue, temple or mosque (p.470).

Understanding the full implications of a networked community can give us hope for the reconstitution of community by connecting people to one another through the use of technology.

Conclusion

The magnet metaphor, which is only one possible metaphor for understanding the organized Jewish community, is a valuable organizational metaphor in that it focuses attention on the needs of institutions and their allocation of their human and financial resources. However, using the magnet metaphor to continue to shape organizational policies and programs is likely to contribute to making Jewish institutions irrelevant to the vast majority of individual Jews. At best, it will stifle responsiveness by letting organizations do the "new" while using old principles of organization; at worst, it will only enable institutions to do the "old" in new ways.

Trying to maintain a limiting organizational metaphor is not an act of leadership. Leadership really requires a balance between a carefully articulated vision of Jewish life and a responsiveness and adaptation to individual needs. As Pearson (1999) notes, "Organizations exist for people and their purposes. They exist to serve people, not the other way around."

It appears that if responsiveness and adaptation do not come from the institutional "core," they are likely to emerge from the individuals on the "periphery." However, leaders of Jewish institutions still have an opportunity to engage *more* individual Jews *more* deeply in a rich Jewish life. That can happen if they are willing to include new models of Jewish community, like the network model, in their thinking, policy-making and programming.

Acknowledgements

The author would like to acknowledge the kindness and collegiality of Dr. Gerald Bubis, Sandy Cardin, Allan Finkelstein, Mort Lowenthal, Gil Mann, Herman Markowitz, Dr. Norman Pearson, Barry Shrage, Rabbi Alan Silverstein, and Dr. Christopher Winship for sharing their insights. Special thanks go to Dr. David Gordis, Rabbi Zachary Heller, and Dr. Jonathan Woocher for carefully critiquing this paper and for organizing a joint JESNA and Wilstein Institute for Jewish Policy Studies symposium around this paper and a Wilstein Institute seminar at Florida Atlantic University. Their wisdom and experience are reflected throughout this paper.

References

Alter, C. and Hage, J. (1993). *Organizations Working Together*. Newbury Park, Calif.: Sage Publications.

Barker, J. (1993). *Paradigms: The Business of Discovering the Future.* New York: HarperCollins.

Brodie, R. (1996). *Virus of the Mind: The New Science of the Meme.* Seattle: Integral Press.

Bubis, G. (June 2000). Setting the terms of reference: Daniel J. Elazar's impact on American Jewish organizational life. *Jerusalem letter,* 432, 1–4.

Cohen, S. and Eisen, A. (1998). *The Jew Within: Self, Community and Commitment Among the Variety of Moderately Affiliated* [Report]. Los Angeles: Susan and David Wilstein Institute of Jewish Policy Studies.

Dawkins, R. (October 8, 2000). What is a Meme? [online]. Alt.memes. Available: http://maxwell.lucifer.com/virus/alt.memetics/what.is.html.

Dent, H. (1998). *The Roaring 2000s: Building the Wealth and Lifestyle You Desire in the Greatest Boom in History*. New York: Simon and Schuster.

Elazar, D. (1997). Jewish Political Studies as a Field of Inquiry. In G. Bubis, D. Elazar, and M. Silberman (Eds.), *Serving the Jewish Polity: The Application of Jewish Political Theory to Jewish Communal Practice.* Philadelphia: Jerusalem Center for Public Affairs and Center for Jewish Communal Studies.

———. (1995). The Federation Movement in Three Contexts: American Jewry, the Jewish Political Tradition, and Modernity. *Jewish Political Studies Review, 7,* 1–12.

———. (1995). *Community and Polity: The Organizational Dynamics of American Jewry* (2nd ed.). Philadelphia: Jewish Publication Society. First edition, 1976, Jewish Publication Society. The 2nd, revised edition is cited in this text.

Elazar, D. and Gerstenfeld, M. (November 1999). A New Agenda for the Jewish People. *Jerusalem Letter, 417,* 1–8.

Eoyang, G. (1997). *Coping with Chaos. Seven Simple Tools.* Cheyenne, Wyo.: Lagumo Corporation.

Friedman, T. (2000). *The Lexus and the Olive Tree* (Rev. ed.). New York: Anchor Books.

Fukuyama, F. (1999). The Great Disruption: Human nature and the Reconstitution of Social Order. *Atlantic Monthly,* review, *283,* 55–80.

Gates, B. (1999). *Business @ The Speed of Thought: Succeeding in the Digital Economy.* New York: Warner Books.

Gergen, K. (1991). *The Saturated Self: Dilemmas of Identity in Contemporary Life.* New York: Basic Books.

Horowitz, B. (2000). *Connections and Journeys: Assessing Critical Opportunities for Enhancing Jewish Identity* [Report]. New York: UJA-Federation of New York.

Israel, S. (2000). The Geometry of Jewish Life. *Journal of Jewish Communal Service, 76,* 261–264.

———. (November 9, 1999). Ethnicity, Geography and Jewish Community [online]. Available: http://www.syn2000.org/Articles/Israel1/Israel1.html.

Kosmin, B. A., Goldstein, S., Waksberg, J., Lerer, N., Keysar, A., and Scheckner, J. (1990). *Highlights of the CJF 1990 National Jewish Population Survey* [Report]. New York: Council of Jewish Federations.

Kuhn, T. (1996). *The Structure of Scientific Revolutions* (3rd ed.). Chicago: University of Chicago Press.

Lipnack, Jessica and Stamps, Jeffrey (1994). *The Age of the Network: Organizing Principles for the 21st Century.* Essex Junction, Vt.: OMNEO.

Merry, Uri. Nonlinear Organizational Dynamics [online]. Retrieved November 1999 from the World Wide Web: http://pw2.netcom.com/~nmerry/art2.htm.

Morgan, G. (1998). *Images of Organizations*. Executive Edition. (2nd ed.). San Francisco: Berrett-Koehler Publishers.

North American Commission on Jewish Identity and Continuity (1995). *To Renew and Sanctify. A Call to Action* [Report]. New York: Council of Jewish Federations and Jewish Education Services of North America.

Pearson, N. (1999). Beyond the Self-defeating Organization. Unpublished manuscript, Capella University.

Petzinger, T. (1999). *The New Pioneers: The Men and Women Who Are Transforming the Workplace and Marketplace*. New York: Simon and Schuster.

Podolny, J. and Page, K. (1998). Network Forms of Organizations. *Annual Review of Sociology*, 24, 54–76. Palo Alto, Calif.: Annual Reviews, Inc.

Powell, W. (1990). Neither Market Nor Hierarchy: Network Forms of Organization. *Research in Organizational Behavior*, 12, 295-336.

Putnam, R. (2000). *Bowling Alone: The Collapse and Revival of American Community*. New York: Simon and Schuster.

Sales, A. and Tobin, G. (Eds.). (1995). *Church and Synagogue Affiliation: Theory, Research and Practice*. Westport, Conn.: Greenwood Press.

Waters, M. (1990). *Ethnic Options: Choosing Ethnic Identities in America*. Berkeley: University of California Press.

Wertheimer, J., Liebman, C., and Cohen, S. (1996). How to Save American Jews. *Commentary*, 47–51.

Woocher, J. (1999). If You Build It, Will They Come? Accessibility, Affordability and Participation in Jewish Communal Life. (Policy paper series). Los Angeles: The Center for Policy Options.

Zemke, R., Raines, C., and Filipczak, B. (2000). *Generations at Work: Managing the Clash of Veterans, Boomers, Xers, and Nexters in Your Workplace*. New York: Amacon.

The Fingerprints of God:
The Community, the Federation,
and the Networks That
Bind Us Together

Barry Shrage

These are the days of miracle and wonder . . .
This is the long distance call. (Paul Simon)

What is a miracle? How are we to understand the call? Rabbi Larry
Kushner describes a miracle and it looks remarkably like a network:

> *Life is supercharged, permeated and over-brimming with purpose and*
> *meaning. Most of the time we are oblivious to it. We go about our lives*
> *as if every event were an accident. And then something happens and we*
> *see the connection. For just a moment it is unmistakable. We are aston-*
> *ished that we couldn't see it until now. All Creation is one great unity.*
> *There are no coincidences.*
>
> *Throughout all Creation, just beneath the surface, joining each person*
> *to each other person and to each other thing in a luminous organism of*
> *sacred responsibility, we discover invisible lines of connection.*

When we look down at our lives from a distance, we see a network of
connecting lines that bind our community and us together, that give
meaning and direction to our lives. Then we realize that these lines are
really the fingerprints of God, the sign of God's involvement in the world,
and then we hear the long distance call.

Three years ago Boston's Federation (CJP) developed a new Strategic
Plan that envisioned radical changes in our Federation and in our community. Today, our community is experiencing a vast increase in Jewish
education with heightened excitement about day schools, synagogues,
family education and adult learning. More social justice and new inner
city projects developed by our dynamic Jewish Community Relations
Council link over 700 Boston Jews through synagogues, Hillels and
schools to our great Jewish commitment to *Tikkun Olam*. There is a significant increase in programs connecting talented, creative people and ini-
tiatives in Boston to our brothers and sisters in Haifa and

Dnepropetrovsk, Ukraine. Underneath it all is the beginning of a new sense of community; a pervasive network that holds all of this together and provides a sense of overall meaning and direction.

But, our Strategic Plan did one more thing that we are just beginning to absorb. The Committee on Vibrancy and Inclusiveness actually suggested a new structure, a new metaphor for our organization and for Jewish life; not a "Federation" of service organizations, but a network linking face-to-face communities and new ideas; agencies and new synagogue partners; community resources and grassroots energy; donors and projects. We are learning to rethink the old Federation model of fundraising and allocations. More than that, we are helping to weave a web of community connection and caring.

Our central premise is that our Jewish people can most helpfully be viewed as an interconnected network of people, communities, ideas, values, culture and knowledge. It is a miraculous network; spanning the entire planet and linking generations across time, as well as human communities across vast geographical distances. Moreover, it is an open network that absorbs ideas, values and culture from the world and shares them again with the world, transformed through contact with Jewish consciousness and experience. The network has practical implications (it has provided the basis for our Jewish identity and Jewish commitment for 3500 years) and also provides a key to our unique Jewish spiritual heritage.

If the network of connections among Jews through personal and institutional relationships define Jewish life and Jewish vibrancy across physical space, Torah (defined broadly as our entire intellectual, literary, spiritual and cultural heritage) defines the content of our existence over time. The metaphor of Jewish learning as a vast interconnected and cross-referenced conversation transcending time and space emerges clearly in Jonathan Rosen's beautiful *The Talmud and the Internet*:

> *I have often thought, contemplating a page of Talmud, that it bears a certain uncanny resemblance to a home page on the Internet, where nothing is whole in itself but where icons and text boxes are doorways through which visitors pass into an infinity of cross-referenced texts and conversations. Consider a page of Talmud. There are a few lines of Mishnah, the conversation the Rabbis conducted (for hundreds of years before it*

was codified around 2000 C. E.) about a broad range of legalistic questions stemming from the bible but ranging into a host of other matters as well. Underneath these few lines begins the Gemarah, the conversation later Rabbis had about the conversation earlier Rabbis had in the Mishnah. Both the Mishnah and the Gemarah evolved orally over so many hundreds of years that, even in a few lines of text, Rabbis who lived generations apart participate and give the appearance, both within those discrete passages as well as by juxtaposition on the page, of speaking directly to each other. The text includes not only legal disputes but fabulous stories, snippets of history and anthropology and biblical interpretations. Running in a slender strip down the inside of the page is the commentary of Rashi, the medieval exegete, commenting on both the Mishnah and the Gemarah, and the biblical passages (also indexed elsewhere on the page) that inspired the original conversation. Rising up on the other side of the Mishnah and the Gemarah are the tosefists, Rashi's descendants and disciples, who comment on Rashi's work, as well as on everything Rashi commented on himself. The page is also cross-referenced to other passages of the Talmud, to various medieval codes of Jewish law (that of Maimonides, for example), and to the Shulkhan Arukh, the great sixteenth century codification of Jewish law by Joseph Caro. And one should add to this mix the student himself, who participates in a conversation that began over two thousand years ago.

Understanding the nature of this 2000-year old network of ideas and our own place in the conversation can inform our ideas about Jewish communities, synagogues, Federations and Federation fundraising campaigns. It provides our communal life with meaning and direction, content and beauty. It teaches us the stories that we tell our children that are the source of our communal culture and our ethical values. And it is self-renewing and filled with change because each generation participates in the discussion and helps define its meaning.

As the late Rabbi Joseph B. Soloveitchik put it:

The prayerful charity community rises to a higher sense of communion in the teaching community, where teacher and dis-

ciple are fully united. The central figure in Jewish history has not been the king, nor the field marshall, nor the political leader, but the very old teacher surrounded by very young children. What does the teacher do? The teacher tells a story. We tell the children the story of laws, which form the foundation of Jewish morality; we tell them the story of honesty and sincerity, love and sympathy; this story is meant to teach the child not to steal, not to lie, not to be vindictive.

In short, it is an exciting story that we tell them. Our story unites countless generations. Present, past, and future merge into one great experience . . . Our story tells of a glorious past that is still real, because it has not vanished, a future which is already here, and a creative present replete with opportunity and challenge. It is a privilege and a pleasure to belong to such a prayerful, charitable, teaching community, which feels the breath of eternity.

The Change Imperative: Rebuilding Community in the 21st Century

From the beginning, the Federation experiment in America has been marked by change. Its success can be measured by the ability of Federation leadership to confront the changing needs of the Jewish people and develop strategies, fund new programs, or support existing or new institutions capable of meeting new challenges. Its long-term ability to attract human and financial resources emerged from its ability to provide leadership, to understand the community's needs and aspirations and to remain at the leading edge of Jewish history.

In 1895, the Federation idea emerged in Boston within the context of community. Those who wrote the first constitution assumed the existence of a self-conscious community with a strong sense of identity and a value system that would support its work. The plan it developed for coordinating the work of agencies caring for a growing immigrant population met a real need and strengthened the pre-existing sense of community through strong and visible action. It built the foundation for the Federation of the future by reaching out to the immigrants who would inevitably move from recipients of aid to leaders, givers and fund-raisers in their own right. It was not created as a "fund raising" organization; it was created with the expectation that by *better meeting emerging needs*, it would "merit more generous support from the community."

Our challenges today are similar to the challenges of the past, but at the same time they are radically different. As always, the Federation's mission includes a deep concern for the needs of vulnerable Jews at home and throughout the world and, as it has from the beginning of the century, a commitment to improving and funding Jewish education in many forms. What has changed, however, is the sense of community upon which the Federation was built when it began its work more than one hundred years ago. In 1895, our sense of community was built on a shared ethnic heritage and a deeply rooted memory of life in the cities and *"shtetlach"* of Europe. It was informed by Jewish values that were a deeply rooted part of the culture learned or inherited by our parents from their immigrant parents. These values supported and directed our communal enterprise, and our sense of community provided the glue that held the *landsmanschaften*, synagogues, and communal aid organizations of the early 20th century together and provided them with their sense of meaning and direction.

For the first seventy years of our existence, our Federation mechanism survived and flourished by focusing on the all-consuming task of meeting the basic needs of our people and helping the first and second generation of immigrants successfully integrate into American society. For the last thirty years, while continuing to meet basic local needs and expanding services to burgeoning "special needs" populations, we focused on the critical challenge of rescuing Jews throughout the world and the wonderful adventure of establishing the Jewish state after 2000 years of exile.

The change that we are confronting at the beginning of the new century involves the slow deterioration of the very glue that binds our community together. Our understanding of Jewish culture, values, history, spirituality and learning have deteriorated under the impact of modernity, materialism, and assimilation that are an integral part of the American experience. While the programs and institutions that we nurtured and developed during the first one hundred years of the Federation's existence provided a superb mechanism for raising the first generation of Jews into the American middle class, and while our efforts overseas helped to rescue millions of Jews and establish the State of Israel, they were never designed to cope with the challenge of assimilation or the deterioration of our sense of community. This is perhaps the most complex, subtle and critical challenge we have ever faced. Without our identity, without a self-conscious sense of community, it becomes difficult or impossible to sustain Jewish life or overcome challenges that our Jewish people have confronted in the past or may confront in the future. Our challenge today must therefore include the development of partnerships and networks that create, sustain, strengthen and re-establish this sense of community and the shared values and common culture that make real communities meaningful, vibrant and viable.

Since 1989, the American Jewish community has been pre-occupied by two concerns. The first is a vision of children and grandchildren who are no longer Jews, who belong to other faiths, or no faith at all, who know little or nothing about their 3500 year-old cultural/spiritual/literary heritage, and who feel little attraction to Jewish institutions or values. The second is a prediction of collapsing institutions, declining campaigns, and the disintegration of the central umbrella institutions of Jewish life. These two nightmares are one. Strongly identified communities will create strong institutions and campaigns, just as weak communities will create weak institutions and weak campaigns.

As in 1895, we now have an opportunity to meet newly emerging needs and, as in 1895, we have a responsibility to reach out, to engage a new group that is not yet part of our community. In 1895, the "new group" was an immigrant generation, our parents and grandparents. Today, the "new group" includes uncommitted and committed Jews who know little about Jewish community and both inmarried and intermarried Jews who are rapidly losing a connection to Jewish life, Jewish values, Jewish culture and Jewish learning. Today, these are our own children and grandchildren. As in 1895, the Federation movement now has an opportunity and responsibility to reach out through our traditional agencies, synagogues and grassroots centers of Jewish energy, with services and programs so that this next alienated generation can, someday, also become part of a Jewish community filled with joy, meaning and purpose.

But how shall we accomplish these complex and critical objectives? Assimilation seems to be the price of modernity and Jewish communities have a frightening tendency to disintegrate in the fourth generation that lives in freedom rather than oppression. Yet this is not the first time we have confronted modernity. From the time of Abraham, to the exile in Egypt, to the era of the judges, kings and prophets, to the challenges of Hellenization and the Roman Empire, we have always found innovative ways to survive and flourish and create renaissance out of disintegration. In each of these periods, indeed, in every period of Jewish history, each generation of Jews faces its own "modernity" and finds its own path to renewal. In our times, this struggle will take as much energy, effort, intelligence, resources, and planning as has our miraculous integration into the American mainstream or the miracle of the creation of the State of Israel.

Face-to-Face Community: The Heart of the Communal Network

The idea of community is at the heart of the Jewish enterprise and a clear definition of community must therefore be the starting point for a renaissance of Jewish life and of the Federation movement. While Federations have sometimes characterized themselves as "the community" and the Federation campaign as the ultimate "community building" experience, it is clear that we require a better definition. If the Federation is to become a network of human energy, linking Jewish communities and individual Jews with ideas and resources, we must begin with a clear definition of community. According to Robert Bellah in *Habits of the Heart:*

> . . . *a community is a group of people who are socially interdependent, who participate together in discussion and decision making, and who share certain practices that both define the community and are nurtured by it. Such a community is not quickly formed. It almost always has a history and so it is also a community of memory.*

> . . . *While the idea of community, if limited to neighbors and friends, is an inadequate basis for meeting our current needs, we want to affirm community as a cultural theme that calls us to wider and wider circles of loyalty, ultimately embracing that universal community of all beings.* . . .

Professor Arnold Eisen translates this idea of community into Jewish terms in his 1995 essay, *"Reimagining Jewish Community in America"* and suggests three starting points or primary building blocks for the definition and construction of Jewish community.

- *It must be local, face-to-face, as near as the re'a or neighbor whom Leviticus 19 commands me to treat in a manner befitting love.*

- *It must also be le'olam: unbounded by time or space, grounded in the unique Jewish situation that is writ large in the world today as much as ever, and dedicated to a tikkun that is commensurably all-embracing.*

- *Finally, on each of those levels, the "words" we speak as Jews must conform to the grammar of Jewish life, underlying and flowing from the conversation begun at Sinai. It must be founded on the Torah, that is to say, based on narrative or resulting in just action. It must include both study and deed — study as deed, deed as study; both of them arising out of community, constituting community and reinforcing community. We will be a community defined by our conversation and our activities.*

Jewish Community in a Mobile World

But how can we maintain "real" Jewish communities in the face of the breathtaking mobility of the 21st century? Paradoxically, I believe that this challenge actually represents our greatest opportunity. How many of us have experienced the beauty and the sense of relief we feel when we find Jewish life in a foreign country we are visiting? Suddenly we are "at home." In a time of mobility, community becomes that much more important, that much more desperately sought after by human beings who are, after all, biologically designed for community existence. The existence of strong, caring communities that will welcome and care about us, wherever we move, becomes that much more important and that much more attractive for Jewish life in the 21st century.

Core Values and A Common Agenda that Binds Us Together

Strong communities are built on common values and a common history, that together, become the "memory" of the community. Likewise, strong values can only develop in the context of a genuine community. Without a powerful, meaningful and inspiring vision of Jewish life, our institutions and communities cannot compete successfully for the hearts and minds of those who can now choose to affiliate with hundreds of exciting and engaging alternatives available in the larger community. We must know what we stand for if we are to offer powerful options.

As diverse as our community is, a set of core beliefs and an action agenda is emerging around which the vast majority of Jews can agree. There is a growing consensus on the importance of developing a renaissance of Jewish community around the basic values and principles of *Torah*—serious Jewish learning; *Chesed*—kindness, and caring for Jews here, in Israel and throughout the Diaspora, and *Tzedek* that is *Tikkun Olam*—social justice and the possibility of a rebuilt world for our Jewish people and for all humankind.

Communities of Learning and Culture—*Torah*

A community that has no cultural, intellectual or spiritual memory has no future. Our community has reached broad agreement about the need to vastly expand Jewish literacy and learning and facilitate a Jewish cultural renaissance through increased support for formal and informal Jewish education for people of all ages and increased attention to emerging institutions of Jewish culture. Small face-to-face communities, particularly synagogues, already educate most of our community's children. But they can be much more. They can become in Isa Aron's words, "congregations of learners" and the central carrier of culture and learning for us and our children.

By surrounding ourselves with learning, particularly sophisticated and comprehensive adult education, we can change the norms of Jewish life and the attitudes we transmit to our children. But the inverse is also true. The process of learning together itself creates community. For the Jewish people, learning can be an intimate act of self-discovery that strengthens the ties that bind us together. Our communities can create opportunities for learning just as learning itself creates community.

Communities of Caring—*Chesed*

The creation of compassionate, face-to-face communities through which we care for each other by visiting the sick, comforting the bereaved, aiding those in need, clearly represents a core agenda for Jewish life. This also includes support for broader community-wide systems of caring such as those provided through our Federation system of services for families, elderly, new immigrants, the sick or people with disabilities here, in Israel and around the world. But it must also include a new focus on our face-to-face communities that are the heart of our communal network.

A thoughtful Harvard Business School case study focuses on the success of the Willow Creek Community Church outside Chicago. That church is now among the most successful in the country, but at the start, it was failing. Market research revealed its core failure as a community. Members felt uncared for and unwelcome. They felt that the Church was more interested in their money than in them as people. This may also be true for most synagogues and communal institutions and it will only get worse as the demand for resources increases.

Change will require a radical new focus on "welcome" and "caring" as core values of Jewish life. For this to happen, the "normal" "*Chesed* committees" of synagogue life will require far more work, attention and resources, and a far greater emphasis on volunteerism. The Willow Creek Community Church had 7000 volunteers under the guidance of 100 professional staff to create a sense of real caring and community for its 30,000 members. It did not happen by accident. While our synagogues and centers (thankfully) operate on a much smaller scale, the development of caring communities that welcome new members, care for the sick, support the disabled, comfort the bereaved and befriend the lonely will require a whole new professional and volunteer structure. It will also require a new relationship between our communal caring agencies (local family services and vocational services) and our gateway face-to-face communities (synagogues and JCCs). In that way, the power and resource of our agency system can inform and strengthen the volunteer networks that can provide support and caring in the communities where people actually live and where the process of face-to-face community building actually takes place.

Communities of Justice—*Tzedek*

A Jewish community that focuses solely on its own needs ignores its most basic historical, Biblical and prophetic mandate. The pursuit of *Tikkun Olam*, social action, the repair of the world for our neighbors and for all humankind, is a third major strategic direction for community building. This value must guide our work to actively involve Jewish adults, college students and teens in advocacy and service projects that engage them in advocacy and building meaningful partnerships that bridge the gap between our largely suburban Jewish community and the city neighborhoods that surround us. This hands-on social justice work should be grounded in a particularly Jewish context, but should be universally applied to carrying out our sacred task of helping to make the world a better place. Community relations councils can be looked to in new ways as coordinating vehicles for engaging synagogues, JCCs, day schools and campus Hillels in carrying out this vision.

The Community Matrix

The Jewish conception of learning, caring and justice can only be fully realized in the context of strong, interdependent "face-to-face" communities. Learning, justice and caring are the very point of Jewish life. They are the seeds of Jewish community. At the same time, Jewish communities are the ground within which these seeds must grow. Too often in the past, strategies for Jewish education/continuity have ignored the need for community, while strategies for community-building have failed to understand that communities require culture, meaning and purpose to flourish. The need for a strategy that supports both must be at the core of the work of our new Federation, our Jewish communal networks.

Federations have a central role to play in community building, but cannot reach out to every member of the Jewish community and cannot become a "face-to-face" community for any but a minority of committed volunteers. For the rest, the task of binding Jews to each other with caring, concern and love, and to systems of Jewish belief, Jewish learning, Jewish values and Jewish social action belong to "gateway" institutions primarily congregations and JCCs. The primary role of these "gateway" institutions is to build community and service their own members, but few of them are designed, organized, funded or staffed to meet the special challenge we face at the beginning of the 21st century. The role of Federation must therefore be to strengthen and support the gateway institutions; to link them to the resources of Federation agencies; to encourage, develop, and fund powerful programs that can truly transform them into communities of *Torah, Tzedek* and *Chesed.*

An Inclusive Vision of Community

Jewish community in America is not singular, but plural. It is made up of hundreds of smaller, more personally engaging communities that can provide avenues of connection to other Jews, opportunities for mutual support and caring, spiritual searching, Jewish learning and cultural activities. By linking existing and emerging communities to each other and to social service agencies and other communal resources, we can enhance their ability to engage and involve people in Jewish life.

Inclusiveness and meaningful involvement must be the hallmarks of these renewed communities. We must reach out to and engage people from all backgrounds and experiences in Jewish communal life. In particular, the communities we envision will be open and welcoming to all. They will be respectful and tolerant of differences and the variety of ways people express their Jewish identity. The Jewish community must be a big tent, open to all. Our communities must be democratic in structure, foster engagement and commitment, and make the best use of the talents, intelligence and ability of all their members.

The Federation Network: Strengthening Gateways to Jewish Community; Assisting Grassroots Institutions; Enhancing Emerging Centers of Jewish Energy; Creating a Community of Communities

Vibrant Jewish communities are enhanced by vibrant, creative, supportive Federations: umbrella institutions that support gateway communities; bind communities together and symbolize *"K'lal Yisroel"* the community of Israel, providing Jewish unity for the Jewish people. Indeed grassroots organizations, synagogues and JCCs, need the Federation to create a "community of communities" as much as Federations need "real communities" to create the basic building blocks of Jewish life. Synagogues, JCCs and other "gateway" communities need Federations to create a "community of communities" in order to broaden their vision, prevent them from becoming narrow and parochial, and enable their members to feel and understand that they are part of a broader Jewish community linking Jews in every synagogue and organization to a broader, more inclusive, network that includes Jews in other organizations; unaffiliated Jews throughout the greater community; the entire American Jewish community; the world Jewish community and ultimately the community which Robert Bellah describes as the "community of all humankind." The new Federation/Network therefore becomes the key connector between local grassroots organizations and the broader Jewish world without which Judaism loses much of its meaning and power.

To meet the needs of a larger and more inclusive Jewish community and to be a real presence, a real "central address," a real "community of communities," I would suggest that Federations and their national organizations must begin to look more like networks than concentric circles or pyramids. Information and funds must flow through these networks, connecting donors and needs; recipients and givers. Knowledge, ideas and vision must replace emergencies, power, money and coercion as the primary forces that hold communities together. In the future the most powerful and influential federations will be those that favor autonomy and that give power away, rather than those that hold power and dominate their systems. Partnerships will replace the traditional benefactor/beneficiary relationship as the most common organizing principle of Federation life.

Enhancing Centrality by Sharing Power and Resources

Throughout the first one hundred years of Federation service to American Jewry, change itself has been the hallmark of our organization's strength and continuity. What began as a federation of a small group of agencies expanded to include new agencies to meet new needs. Older agencies merged or disappeared and the Federation expanded to meet overseas needs as well. At each stage of development, the existing agencies showed a willingness to share resources for the general benefit of the Jewish people. Each time the Federation opened its doors to new groups, each time it shared power and resources, its centrality and influence grew. Throughout its first one hundred years, the Federation served the community best by providing a common vision, a sense of unity, the strength to confront real emergencies and crises, and, most importantly, the ability to facilitate the development of new services to meet new needs by bringing ideas, institutions and human and financial resources together in new ways. The ability to share power and resources and to bring ideas, communities and resources together in new ways is at the heart of the network idea.

The Jewish Network: Implications for the Future of the Federation

1. **Connecting Jews: The Tipping Point and the Power to Make Change.** Boston is a community of 200,000 Jews. Too large perhaps to be a "real" community and much larger than the far more intimate world of Cleveland's Jewish community where I worked for nine years. And yet after about five years I had gotten to know almost every Rabbi of most of Boston's larger congregations and many of the smaller congregations as well. I also had a connection of some kind to almost every name that emerged in conversations with a wide range of community members. All of this would be a forgone conclusion in Cleveland with 70,000 Jews and perhaps impossible in New York with a Jewish population of 1.5 million, but I was pleasantly surprised that I was beginning to develop connections to many parts of Boston's Jewish community "network."

Several years ago, I attended a funeral of a woman who was well known and well liked, but far from the best known woman in our Boston Jewish community. About 300 people came and I began to consider what this meant to the idea of connections among Jews. If this great lady knew at least 300 people, and if each of those people were connected one way or another to at least another 100 people, then it seemed realistic to believe that almost any Jew in Boston was less than two degrees of separation from any other Jew, no matter how apparently distant. To put it simply, it was quite possible that an apparently "alienated," "distant," "unaffiliated," or "unreachable" Jew living in Westboro (far from the Center of Jewish Boston) could well be the cousin or friend of the president of a synagogue in Brookline (at the heart of Jewish Boston!) This idea has enormous implications for challenges as diverse as outreach to intermarried households and Federation campaigns. "Alienation" and "distance" suddenly become much more relative in a "network" conception of community.

The Jewish community is far more tightly connected than most of us believe. Even the most alienated Jews are probably not much more than two degrees of separation from the most affiliated. Moreover, these states are highly dynamic as people move between levels of connection depending on their place in the family lifecycle and their relationships with influentials who connect them to the Jewish community and who also influence their attitudes.

The Network concept, and the close connection between affiliated and unaffiliated Jews that it suggests, also challenges the idea that the community consists of disconnected concentric circles with committed Jews at the core and unaffiliated, "unreachable" Jews at the periphery. This is the central insight developed by Rabbi Hayim Herring in his excellent paper, "Network Judaism: A New Image for Understanding the Organization of American Jews," prepared for a Wilstein Institute symposium on the network idea. Rabbi Herring's network concept provides a far more flexible and nuanced roadmap of the American Jewish community with far more potential for outreach to alienated groups of all kinds.

The Tipping Point, by Malcolm Gladwell, provides additional critical insight into the networks that tie our lives and our communities together. He suggests ways that those can be "tipped," changing attitudes and reshaping social reality structures. He describes three "rules of epidemics:" "the law of the few;" "the stickiness factor;" and "the power of context." He believes that by understanding these factors we can change the social reality in which we live. In his words, "little things can make a big difference."

> *What must underlie successful social change in the end is a*
> *bedrock belief that change is possible, that people can radically*
> *transform their behavior or beliefs in the face of the right*
> *kind of impetus. This too contradicts some of the most*
> *ingrained assumptions we hold about each other and ourselves.*
> *We like to think of ourselves as autonomous and inner directed*
> *that who we are and how we act is something permanently set*
> *by our genes and our temperament. {But . . . if you add up*
> *the examples found in* The Tipping Point,*} they amount to*
> *a very different conclusion about what it means to be human.*
> *We are actually powerfully influenced by our surroundings,*
> *our immediate context, and the personalities of those around*
> *us. . . . That's why social change is so volatile and so often*

inexplicable because it is the nature of all of us to be volatile and inexplicable.

But if there is difficulty and volatility in the world of The Tipping Point, *there is a large measure of hopefulness as well. Merely by manipulating the size of a group, we can dramatically improve its receptivity to new ideas. By tinkering with a presentation of information, we can significantly improve its stickiness. Simply by finding and reaching those few special people who hold so much social power, we can shape the course of social change. In the end, Tipping Points are a reaffirmation of the potential for change and the power of intelligent action. Look at the world around you. It may seem like an immovable, implacable place. It is not. With the slightest push—in just the right place, it can be tipped.*

Is this not exactly our challenge? Somehow we are called upon to join in a revolution that must reshape the attitudes of a generation hungry for meaning, but not knowing where to find it and searching for community, and not knowing quite how to create it. As part of this larger struggle we are testing the proposition that our Federation movement has a role to play in this great adventure. At the heart of Gladwell's idea is "the law of the few." He suggests that our society is tied together by relatively few "connectors;" really key influentials who seem to know everybody and who carry messages and ideas across vast distances with amazing speed and accuracy. He also describes "mavens" who seem to know everything and who carry the content of these ideas and "salespeople" who close the sale and drive the new ideas home. Federations control vast financial resources but they also influence even more potent human resources. By understanding these human resources and the way they and communal agencies and institutions connect our "community network," we can strengthen communal life and help drive the revolution of *"Torah, Tzedek* and *Chesed"* upon which the future of Jewish communal life can be built. And if the Federation movement is successful, if it can be seen as having been a critical part of this process, it will be visible and "central" in a way it has not been since 1973.

2. Connecting Jews: The Tipping Point and the Power to Communicate. Communicating the Federation "idea" is one of our most difficult challenges. How many times have we heard Federation leadership say, "We could raise much more money if people only knew all the good we do." But, communicating a complex message is far more difficult than it seems. Traditional solutions like advertising, through electronic or print media do not seem to work and are far too expensive for the amount of repetition required to truly communicate a complex message.

The network model suggests different options. Several years ago, during our strategic planning process, Professor Leonard Schlesinger (then at the Harvard Business School) reminded us that we are not AT & T or IBM and certainly cannot use communications strategies that were designed to increase market share by one or two points in a target audience of tens of millions with thousands of repetitions in the electronics and print media. Most Federations already reach twenty to thirty percent of their "target audience" and the rest is fairly clearly defined. We actually know half of the people that we are seeking to reach and the rest are closely tied by "invisible," but discoverable "lines of connection." He suggested that a community organization like ours, with a clearly defined geographical constituency, might be more like the "Tupperware Lady" or Amway, communicating far more effectively through "word of mouth" networks and face-to-face neighborhood meetings. This model meshes well with Gladwell's ideas and suggests a possible Federation communication strategy based on "connectors" and "sticky messages" rather than traditional public relations and advertising approaches.

Several years ago, Hebrew College in Boston and CJP created a remarkable adult education program called *Me'ah* (A Hundred Hours of Jewish Learning) modeled loosely on the Wexner Heritage Program (Bible, rabbinics, Jewish history and Jewish philosophy - two years, 25 weeks per year, two and one-half hours in the classroom and two hours of homework per week.) It started with 40 participants and grew to 800 participants per year within four years. The program developed without much advertising or print media, no electronic media and limited direct mail. But, we started the program in its first years in two highly visible, fast growing young affluent congregations and targeted, to the extent possible, younger more visible congregants. The results were extraordinary. The program already has over 1000 graduates and the name,

"*Me'ah*" is recognized not only across Jewish Boston but in other communities as well. Of course, this would not have happened if the Hebrew College had not created an extraordinary product. But the placement strategy and "word-of-mouth" contagion must also be credited with the program's success in the community.

3. **A New Relationship with Donors and A Network of Communal Partners.** It is becoming increasingly clear that a new generation of donors requires, is even demanding, more direct connection to smaller scale, more personal charities with less bureaucracy and more ability to "make a difference." But if "donor choice" is part of the answer, we still need to assure that communal needs are met and that our Federations can continue to generate a sense of overarching community and Jewish peoplehood. In a world of donor choice, what is the "value added" of the Federation? What will our relationship be to our old and new agency partners?

Barry's Magic *Kiddush* Cup: The Funnel and the "Partnership" Network

As a gift on my 50th birthday, my friends and family gave me a special *kiddush* cup. It is a traditional custom that the person making *Kiddush* pours wine from his or her cup for all those at the table who share in his or her blessing. This is often a symbolically beautiful, but aesthetically messy affair. My new silver *Kiddush* cup is an elaborate contraption with a cup at the top sitting in a kind of funnel into which the wine is poured to be distributed through eight silver tubes into eight small silver cups set up in a perfect circle around the "magic" *Kiddush* cup. Our old federation system is very much like my "magic" *Kiddush* cup into which the donor pours his or her money. From the point of view of most donors, decision-making takes place at local federations (or nationally through the UJA) in a "black box" and money flows out the bottom to a number of more or less pre-determined institutions, a classic "benefactor/beneficiary" relationship. It is very neat and the system hardly loses a drop, but the donor does not feel much of a sense of participation. The system we are beginning to develop in Boston is more like a computer network, linking donors and communal needs with local and international agencies and serving more like a central processor, creating vision along with a wide range of partners, nurturing creativity and facilitating change.

The partnership concept is ideally suited to this new world of networks and new relationships. The agency system, as it has functioned over the last one hundred years, is a wonderful communal tool, ever changing and, at least in Boston, extremely dynamic and responsive to the needs of the community. Nevertheless, it is not, and cannot be, the sum total of all communal activity. Meeting needs in the renaissance paradigm requires additional partners and connections, and just as day schools were added to our system fifty years ago, synagogues and other emerging organizations will be added over the next few years. In a world of community involvement and engagement, where we must enable donors to "make a difference," it becomes more and more important for us to connect donors, new agencies, new projects and new opportunities, while at the same time, providing continuing support for our existing system. We believe, and are demonstrating, that careful use of structured designations and our new concept of partnership will enhance our fundraising and provide significant new opportunities for current beneficiaries and new partners alike.

In a partnership both sides give and take. Both sides play an important role. Both sides work together to shape strategy and goals. In our work in Boston, we identified literally hundreds of new groups and programs that desperately wanted a CJP connection. Many of these groups were not even asking for financial support, but simply access to ideas, consultation, fundraising support and participation in communal strategy. As we completed our Strategic Plan, we realized that as we responded to their needs, we were at the same time expanding our connection to the community and *increasing* the size of our "communal network" and our "reach" as a Federation.

The Synagogue Partnership

Synagogues and their congregations are the most widespread form of grassroots communal organization available to American Jews. Surveys show that American Jews continue to feel closer to their congregations than to any other form of Jewish organizational life. Jews of all kinds, inmarried and intermarried, Reform, Conservative, Orthodox, Reconstructionist and unaffiliated, continue to form synagogues largely out of their own volunteer energy, from renewed urban communities to the small synagogues that are forming in developing suburbs. These congregations must further develop their community building capacity before they can fulfill their potential as an important component of a Jewish renaissance, but many are showing surprising energy, reflecting the power of volunteers who are hungry for real community and spiritual meaning in their lives.

Central to the work of the new Federation system and primary to the renaissance process must be a new partnership with the synagogue world. Congregations are not the only locus of community energy, or a significant source of face-to-face community, but they are a massive and widespread system of potential engagement that has for too long stood outside the federation matrix without significant federation support or the benefit of synergy with the federation system. Indeed no significant progress can be made in the work of Jewish Renaissance without the full trust and cooperation of congregations and congregational movements.

Central to our strategy for Jewish renaissance is a process of reinventing and re-envisioning the congregation and the federation to meet rapidly changing needs. The congregation of the 21st century, we have come to believe, must be transformed, as many already have, from a house of prayer, on the one hand, and a school for children on the other, to a total integrated educational environment that brings all the elements and arms of our movements and federations together with one overarching aim: the spiritual/religious/ethical transformation of every Jewish family that passes through the congregational gateway. This cannot be accomplished doing "business as usual" at synagogues or at federations. For congregations to become the source of universal Jewish literacy for adults; caring communities that use and engage volunteer energy; and the critical touchstone for the work of *Tikkun Olam* will require significant new financial resources and a true partnership with federations. For this to happen, the vision and the structure of each will need to change in revolutionary ways.

In Boston, the Commission on Jewish Continuity, a partnership between CJP and its agencies and the congregational movements and their synagogues, has produced exactly this kind of revolution. It has created programs that are bringing vastly increased family education, adult learning, youth work, teacher training, Israel experiences, social action and volunteerism to most congregations in cooperation with Boston's Hebrew College, the JCRC and the Bureau of Jewish Education. It has also developed the Jewish Resource Network Initiative (JRNI) precisely to provide the consultation and support that congregations need to develop the organizational structures required to support this expanded mission and array of vastly increased programming.

How the Network Links Donors and Institutions

• Cooperative Relationships

As our new Federation network moves to support organizations at the grassroots of the Jewish community, we will increasingly find ourselves helping organizations both inside and outside the normal Federation "system of agencies." Federations have traditionally helped their agencies through funding and human resource development; planning through a process that brings agencies, ideas and the intellectual leadership of our community together; and advocacy for government and foundation support. In the process, federations can increasingly be viewed as support systems, facilitators, and consultants for our communal network These kinds of cooperative relationships can be expanded beyond our "system of agencies" to create a much broader communal network, with much greater reach beyond our traditional constituencies.

• Cooperative Fundraising

In addition to funding for specific projects, federations may also provide fundraising support for federation agencies, grassroots organizations and synagogues alike, further blurring the line between cooperators and competitors. Support for these efforts strengthens these agencies and their important work and also increases the perception of the federation's centrality and importance in the community and among major donors who appreciate federation support for programs and agencies for which they care.

In the past, the centrality of federations grew in part out of their ability to serve as a philanthropic conduit, funneling donor resources to a specific pool of beneficiary agencies. As donors demand more choice and a greater connection to philanthropic dollars, federations struggle to maintain their ability to plan while also meeting donor needs and expectations. The notion of co-evolution may provide some ideas for new models that can preserve a clear federation role by better serving "linking institutions" and donors. In fact, Boston's CJP is already informally experimenting with three models in addition to the vitally important traditional role of umbrella fundraising:

• Federation as Philanthropic Advisor

As philanthropic advisor, federations work with donors (frequently through their Personalized Funds) to help them identify programs and meet their philanthropic needs. At the same time, federations have an opportunity to highlight programs that meet overall communal strategic objectives.

• Federation as Philanthropic Network

As the hub of a *"philanthropic network,"* federations serve as a "central processor" to link donors to complex projects involving multiple agencies in which federations have played a role as planner and facilitator. Here, federations play a very different and far more active role linking donors to "systems of services." Federations meet the philanthropic need of the donor, but also play a critical "value added" role by adding ideas or vision or by facilitating cooperation among agencies to address large and complex communal challenges.

• Federation as Fund-Raising Consultant

As *fund-raising consultant* to agencies and grassroots groups, a federation can strengthen its centrality while increasing collaboration and cooperation by supporting, guiding and consulting on fundraising projects. In experimental programs, supporting fundraising activities of several congregations and day schools, CJP seems to have played an effective role, while at the same time adding new donors to Federation rolls and increasing Federation giving among several key donors who appreciated the support for their favorite institutions.

Taken together, all of these provide new ways for us to explore the notion of turning competitors into collaborators in a network designed to strengthen Jewish life in new and innovative ways.

4. The Death of Competition: Re-Engineering the Federation and Its Network Relationships. About two years ago, a federation colleague told me that her federation was "in mourning." The reason was an unexpected and unprecedented multi-million dollar gift to a local day school. "Why," the leadership of the Federation wanted to know "didn't we get that gift?"

What is wrong with this picture? Do we not want that day school to be built? Is the day school really the competition? Must money flow through the communal planning process for it to "count?" Must money flow through the communal planning process to be a true "community" gift? I do not think that anyone would argue anymore that day schools are our "competition" and federation planning is hardly a model of pure rationality. How do we begin to conceptualize a federation in which every good Jewish cause is potentially part of our network and in which few good Jewish causes are "the competition?"

The network idea makes collaborators out of competitors and calls for a renewed partnership that will link our system in new and innovative ways.

James F. Moore, in *The Death of Competition*, reminds us that the key to taking advantage of opportunities in a rapidly changing, fast moving and highly complex world is a new relationship with former competitors:

> *What many companies lack is a framework for positioning themselves to take advantage of these changes rather than be victimized by them.*
>
> *The secret is embracing cooperation, or co-evolution. This is the key to harnessing innovation, to bringing new value to the marketplace and to discovering how each worker can make important contributions to the future.*
>
> *The Intel Corporation provides an interesting model of a company that identifies and embraces new possibilities through co-evolution. Intel is, of course, the maker of the microprocessor engines that power most of our personal computers. It invests*

many billions of dollars each year on chip design and manu-
facturing capability.

But a little-known fact is that it also invests more than
$100 million each year guiding co-evolution across the entire
computer, communications and media landscape.

Through its Intel Architecture Labs based in Oregon, the com-
pany does research on future uses and designs for computing
and communications. It then gives away the fruits of this
research in order to enable other companies to share in bring-
ing these capabilities to market in concert with Intel. Intel
knows that it can't succeed without other companies. So by
embracing them, it creates advantages for the entire industry
and for itself. The industry gets the leadership it needs to
work together. Intel ensures that it will be central to the
future that emerges.

All of this suggests a very different planning and allocation process. In this new world of the Federation/Network planning will take precedence over allocations as larger donors increasingly choose projects identified through federation sponsored collaborative planning processes. Moreover, the planning process itself may look quite different through a network lens.

Jessica Lipnack and Jeffrey Stamps, in their brilliant and groundbreaking book, *The Age of Networks*, suggest five rules for maintaining a true network of partners. Their work has real implications for turning our system of agencies (generally hierarchical benefactor–beneficiary relationships with "our" agencies on the inside and every other institution on the outside) into a true collaborative network spanning the entire community with a very different planning process. The five distinguishing features of our new Federation/Network are:

1. **Unifying Purpose**—A shared commitment to the same goal and a common vision, not legalism and rules, will hold the network together.

2. **Independent Members**—Each agency, synagogue and institution is different. Each must retain its independence while cooperating with others on specific projects.

3. **Voluntary Links**—Our network of agencies, synagogues and institutions should communicate extensively and meet often. No one is forced to participate. There are many crisscrossing relationships.

4. **Multiple Leaders**—Different people and organizations lead depending on what needs to be done. During any given process more than one person leads.

5. **Integrated Levels**—People work at many levels within the Federation and within other partner organizations within the Federation/Network. The Federation/Network is itself embedded in the larger polity in which it exists and as part of a national and international system of Jewish concern.

The Gesher Project, an innovative grassroots young adult outreach program, and CJP's response to the opportunity it presented, provides an example of the network concept. Gesher was developed by and for young adults. It was an idea that was developed independently and entrepreneurially with some support from CJP and with enormous volunteer energy. Gesher independently raised tens of thousands of dollars, used a network model to recruit hundreds of volunteer "mentors" and developed an Internet based strategy to attract thousands of young adults to our community. The leaders and creators were feisty and self-assured, almost arrogant, and represented a very different culture than CJP but they were also enormously effective. To completely absorb them would have been difficult and would have certainly destroyed their entrepreneurial, volunteer driven culture. To have rejected them would have decreased their chances of success and would have cut CJP off from a critical source of human energy and creativity. In the end CJP chose a strategy built on the network models and created a voluntary partnership based on a mutuality of interests and a "unifying purpose." Our strategy preserved Gesher's independence, tied it through "voluntary links" to our other young adult serving agencies and provided funding, support, consultation and facilitation to strengthen the organization and highlight CJP's role at the heart of the network. A careful co-branding plan was also developed.

Toward a New Federation Organizational and Governance Structure

In addition to obvious implications for the Federation's relationship to its traditional agencies and new partners, the Lipnack-Stamps principles also provide important insight into the kinds of internal restructuring that federations require to face their new challenges. Among other opportunities, consider current federation board and committee structures and the possible development of a "networked" organization based on "independent members," "voluntary links," and the other "network principles."

Increasingly we hear dissatisfaction and impatience from younger leadership. They need to be involved in shorter term, higher impact projects. Lengthy processes and committee meetings bore them. They need to bring their expertise to the table, achieve results, feel satisfied, and then go back to their families and their work.

But if governance were reconceptualized to allow meetings to take place as needed, with different participants required to achieve different outcomes, the entire feel of the federation enterprise could change. While many questions remain to be answered, the network conception would seem to provide far more opportunity for new style engagements than our existing structure.

5. **National and Overseas Networks**. Many of the same rules for the creation of domestic networks can be used to create new national and overseas organizations better designed to meet the complex requirements of the twenty-first century. Consider the United Jewish Communities (UJC), our new umbrella national organization, and its need to achieve consensus, overcome paralysis, reduce costs, provide a greater sense of involvement for federation leadership and local federations and link a wide range of national and international enterprises in meeting needs, planning for the future, and creating a sense of "Jewish peoplehood," and international Jewish community. Clearly old style bureaucratic solutions are not working and attempts to create near unanimity for "collective responsibility" have paralyzed the organization at many levels. The creation of a new organizational model based on networks and network principles (unifying purpose, independent members, voluntary links, multi-

ple leaders and integrated levels) could allow our national system to move more quickly on programs that are "voluntarily" agreed upon by "independent" members in a far more "integrated" fashion. Central to this new model, however, would be the development of a clear "unifying purpose."

The central struggle of the Federation system, as it begins its second century, is the development of a new "unifying purpose." A great deal of our intellectual energy must be devoted to open, energizing debate on this issue. There are two very different perspectives on the nature of this vision and the future of the federation movement. Will overseas needs and "sacred survival" continue to be the glue that holds our system together or will we allow the new "renaissance" theme to fully develop? The nature of the vision that emerges to guide our future is not unrelated to the structure that we must create. The old "sacred survival" agenda focused on terrifying overseas crises seemed to require highly centralized fundraising and planning, hierarchical structures and rigid rules all designed to save lives and address ever recurring crises and emergencies. The fundraising and allocations process that emerged from this system was stable and effective, but was also very slow to change and often seemed literally and figuratively frozen and limited. The renaissance agenda, on the other hand, demands more openness, new partners and far more flexibility.

Our international system faces its own complex challenges. The future needs of our international system are quite different than the old emergency driven challenges of the past. Israel, in particular, is now a self-sufficient, highly industrialized society with needs that are quite different from those of previous eras, while the American Jewish community seeks a new basis for a strong international Jewish community based on real relationships rather than "Ari Ben Canaan" stereotypes.

A UJC sponsored seminar in Israel in June 2000 attracted experts from around the world and developed a consensus on the critical challenges facing our international system and the people of Israel. At the heart of almost every analysis was a common understanding of the need to foster Jewish peoplehood by rapidly creating a vast network of real "face-to-face" relationships linking Diaspora and Israeli Jews and Jewish communities around the world. They also outlined the new challenges facing Israel and American society and the new approaches required to meet these challenges. They all highlighted:

- The importance of people-to-people and community-to-community connections as an independent priority for American Jewish investment. Several speakers identified people-to-people and community-to-community partnerships as the highest priority for American Jewish philanthropy in Israel and overseas.

- The need to focus on short-term, high impact projects where American Jewish expertise, as well as human resources could be used to leverage financial resources and provide a significant "value added" for American Jewish involvement.

- The value to Israel and Jewish communities in the former Soviet Union of partnering with American Jews in order to foster mutual sharing and learning, especially with regard to Jewish identity, pluralism, volunteerism, democratic values, and community building.

- The importance of using American Jewish resources to identify unmet needs and new service models; advocate for underserved populations; foster community-based responses to social problems and serve as a catalyst for change.

- The need for American Jewish intellectual and human resources in areas like strategic planning, community development, and grassroots empowerment and the critical importance of delivering service in a way that generates excitement and increased commitment in the American Jewish community.

While some tasks can and should be carried out in a collective way, I would argue that most of these challenges, the kind of challenges we face today, will yield more readily to networked small-scale entrepreneurial programs than to a single collective approach. The notion that networks of smaller scale entrepreneurial efforts can be more efficient than centrally planned large-scale, quasi-governmental efforts in building community, creating civic responsibility, fostering economic change and meeting needs has become increasingly clear to most of us over the last twenty years. This has been reinforced by our experiences in Project Renewal and Partnership 2000. In the Jewish community, our new challenges require the development of increased "social capital" that can both build community and develop multi-faceted highly leveraged funding strategies that provide a "Federation value-added" in creativity, donor connection and access to new resources to meet the challenges of the 21st century.

These needs require far more than traditional centralized planning models can provide. Creativity, leverage, grassroots collaboration and people-to-people relationships are all even more important than financial resources (though financial resources are still critical) to be effective in these critical areas. Imagine instead a national and international system built on "unifying purpose;" "independent members." "voluntary links;" "multiple leaders" and "integrated levels." A new kind of network for a very new set of challenges!

Conclusion: Creating A Tipping Point of Jewish Community and Jewish Meaning

Against all odds the Jewish people have carried a powerful message of hope within a strong communal network for over 2000 years. In a time that lacks vision and prophecy and that yearns for meaning, we are carrying an ancient faith in an ancient God so that our children and grandchildren will have spiritual options to fill their lives with light and joy.

In a time of greed and selfishness, we are part of a very old tradition of caring for strangers, of love of the poor and oppressed, and a responsibility for widows and orphans, the elderly and handicapped.

In a time of forgetfulness, we are part of the oldest living chain of learning and literature in the world, inheritors of an ancient and hauntingly beautiful culture.

In a time of anomie and loneliness, we carry the secret of community making and caring to provide our children and grandchildren a sense of community and belonging.

In a time of rootlessness and alienation we are connecting to a 3500-year-old history and an infinite future.

The Federation movement has a powerful role to play in renewing this message and strengthening and reshaping our communal network. If we carry out this great work with spirit and vision, we will create a tipping point of Jewish learning and community and justice, we will succeed in our great mission, and future generations will bless us for our work and our vision.

ANALYSIS and COMMENTS

David M. Gordis
Christopher Winship
Jonathan S. Woocher
Alan Silverstein
Allan Finkelstein
Neuman F. Pollack

Response and Policy Recommendations
Hayim Herring

David M. Gordis

Thoughts on the Network Judaism Metaphor

Hayim Herring proposes a reconsideration of the regnant metaphor descriptive of the Jewish community, originally introduced by Daniel Elazar in *Community and Polity*. He then proceeds to critique the applicability of the "magnetic core" model to the contemporary Jewish community and proposes a new model, "network Judaism," as a more apt and useful design for the contemporary Jewish community. Barry Shrage describes how that networking model already informs the emerging Jewish community of Boston, where the Combined Jewish Philanthropies has been central in energizing institutions, organizations and interconnections between them to generate a renaissance of Jewish life. Rabbi Alan Silverstein has some serious reservations about the apparently "non-directive" nature of the Herring model but approves of many of the practical inferences from the model to create a more responsive and engaging Jewish community. Christopher Winship and Neuman Pollack take a somewhat more theoretical look at the Herring paper, Winship suggesting the interesting analogy of the Jewish community and the American University which, he claims, may have lost its moral authority precisely because it has become more market-driven and less directive and top-down driven. Pollack places the Herring paper in the larger framework of American ethnicity and raises fundamental issues underlying the more pragmatic and strategic observations and considerations discussed by others.

For both Herring and Shrage, the major implications of the newly proposed metaphor relate to the way organizations function and interrelate. Networking implies a far more user friendly mode of operation than generally prevails in Jewish organizational life. It suggests that synagogues, federations and other Jewish organizations need to be more responsive to the needs of individuals who approach them seeking to engage Jewish life, but to do so on their terms rather those imposed by top-down driven organizational structures and strong centralized leadership. Herring argues that Elazar's "magnets" often do not work, and that there is an ideological content implicit in the core-periphery structure, suggesting that "more is better," and that leadership is pretty sure of what the more should be. Herring's translation of this suggested re-thinking of the metaphor is primarily into terms of organizational style.

The importance of metaphor goes far beyond organizational modalities, however, for metaphor suggests a way of looking at Judaism and Jewish life philosophically and ideologically. The core-periphery metaphor may require revision not simply to shape a more user-friendly institutional and organizational environment for Jews. Organizations should be more responsive to the needs of individuals. They should listen to what people are saying and they should be more efficient and less laden with the excrescencies of bureaucratic structure. Those changes may be well described as introducing a networking style to Jewish organizational life, but they are not dependent on adopting a new metaphor. The new metaphor is far more significant than what it implies for the style of organizational functioning, though the enhancement of organizational responsiveness, which Herring describes as "network Judaism," is certainly desirable and important.

The Elazar model of core and periphery should not be discarded. Herring points out that it is still useful though incomplete. In many cases the magnet does function well. Many of us can relate stories of people who were distant from any sort of engagement with Jewish life whose interest was piqued by contact with a seriously committed Jew. In fact, the impact of personal contact with a person who is seriously engaged with Jewish study, observance and community involvement, may remain the most effective instrument of Jewish re-connection. The new metaphor need not deny the usefulness of "magnetic attraction." It requires revision for other reasons.

The Elazar model was shaped by an earlier and simpler stage of American Jewish life. Answers to fundamental questions seemed clear. Goals and objectives of Jewish public life and personal life appeared to be almost self-evident. Jews who had, to all intents and purposes, abandoned Jewish observance had to be influenced to reconnect with the Synagogue and with Sabbath and holiday observance and the central features of the Jewish personal calendar as well. Israel was the central item on the Jewish public agenda, and Jews whose commitment to financial and political support was tenuous had to be strengthened in their allegiance and encouraged to articulate a strengthened commitment in their daily lives. Jews who had placed the goal of "making it in America" at the center of their lives needed to be reawakened to the compatibility of Judaism and

Americanism. And finally, those whose financial support for the institutions of American Jewish life had waned needed to be brought "back into the fold" of responsible Jewish citizenship, including the philanthropic dimension. These objectives appeared to be clear and self-evident. Jewish leadership, both professional and volunteer, knew what the Jewish community needed and could plan and shape a Jewish community with these goals in mind. They could function with a sense that while success may not have been assured, the way of preparing for the Jewish future was clear and the nature of the "ideal Jew" and optimal Jewish community were known. In this environment, the core-periphery model appeared most serviceable and the "magnet" was a useful metaphor and organizational model for planning the future.

Elazar probably never intended his metaphor to constitute a description of the organizational structure of American Jewish life, rather, he intended to convey the picture of Jewish goals and objectives that I have described. Much of the agenda that emerges from a core-periphery model remains valid. But times have changed; issues are far more complex than they were when Elazar shaped his metaphor, and that is why the metaphor requires revision.

Many things have changed. While Israel remains a major concern for American Jews, particularly at this difficult time, the center of gravity of American Jewish life has shifted to deal with the content of Jewish life for American Jews, or, put somewhat differently, what it means to be a Jew in contemporary America. The simpler mentality of "the world against the Jews," has receded somewhat in a burgeoning of interreligious and intergroup contacts that have attempted to come to terms with the painful and tragic history of these interrelationships and establish a different paradigm of how the world deals with the "otherness" of the other. Highly educated and sophisticated Jews who have found their way back to Jewish learning and Jewish culture are questioning the nature of Jewish belief as they reaffirm their Jewish engagement, rejecting the notion that modernity and Judaism are antithetical and adversarial. Exploring universal human concerns from a Jewish perspective, they are seeking new ways of balancing particular Jewish concerns and universal human values. As participants in the larger culture as well as the Jewish community, Jews are experimenting with new ways of envisioning community and navigating between the poles of individualism and community connection. The very nature of Jewish belief is being reshaped in new forms of religious fellowship, while the future of the traditional Jewish religious denominations remains an open question.

The dilemma faced by the organized Jewish community is that at this time of significant change and fluidity, plans must be made to strengthen the institutional and organizational structures of Jewish life. The current reality of Jewish life, in all its excitement and potential, requires an openness to experimentation and ears and minds attuned to the formulations, approaches, articulated needs and interests of a newly emerging Jewish community. This openness is well expressed in the Network metaphor, which rejects a top-down driven image and seeks insight, wisdom and creativity from all those who engage Jewishly, whether at the center or more peripherally involved, as long as they have the competence to engage their Jewishness and Judaism knowledgeably. But there is an implicit tension between the openness at the base of this network metaphor, and the need for planning which requires centralization, and some degree of direction and bureaucratic leadership style.

The challenge that we face then, in response to the new reality and the suggestion of a reshaped guiding metaphor for Jewish life, is to adopt the revision without abandoning what must be sustained from the earlier formulation. We require openness, but not openness without limit. Jewish institutions need to be responsive to new formulations and newly articulated needs, but at the same time Jewish institutions must continue to convey the values of Jewish tradition that form the foundation of Jewish life and culture. Organizations must enhance their ability to hear and respond, but they must also not abandon their ability to speak from their traditional sources.

The nature of the Jewish community of tomorrow will emerge from the continuing dialogue between the present and the past. Jewish continuity requires the active participation of a literate and engaged Jewish community to inform the process of planning and building for the future. We do not know all the answers. We do not know what Jewishly authentic patterns of belief will emerge as the present generations reexamines the intersection of Judaism with modern life. We do not yet know the shape of Jewish communal structures that will emerge as the community explores anew fundamental issues of values and beliefs. The network model suggests that we should not be alarmed by the current pace of change. Change, after all, is the law of life, and we are part of a living Jewish community. The network metaphor suggests that we allow space in all of our planning for the working out of the dialogue and the experimentation. The tectonic shifts in Jewish life can be the precondition for a new era of Jewish vitality and creativity. Signs of this creativity are evident in Boston and elsewhere. Network Judaism is at the core the admonition to nurture this creativity, nourish it, build from its products and emerge energized and revitalized.

Christopher Winship

The Weakness of Strong Organizations

Rabbi Herring is to be congratulated on writing an important and provocative paper that provides a critical insight into how the American Jewish community works. In particular, he points out that we think about and organize ourselves around a model of concentric circles where strongly affiliated Jews are at the center and more weakly affiliated and attached Jews are in successive rings as one moves out towards the periphery. Of course, this insight is not new. In fact, part of the evidence that Herring puts forth in support of his claim is Daniel Elazar's description of the American Jewish community as working precisely in this way in his book, *Community and Polity: The Organizational Dynamics of American Jewry*. However, as Mary Douglas points out in her classic book, *How Institutions Think*, almost no one ever has a novel idea, rather, genius exists in being able to demonstrate the importance and relevance of an idea at the critical time and place. This is what Rabbi Herring has done. Furthermore, in true Douglasian fashion, he demonstrates that the concentric model may not so much describe how we are in fact organized, as Elazar argued, but rather that it is the model we use in our thinking about institutional structure. Most appropriately, Herring points out that other models might both be more empirically accurate and normatively more successful as Jews seek to understand, maintain and expand their community.

Herring's analysis points to a more general set of issues: the weakness of strong organizations. This is an issue that Albert Hirschman has analyzed in depth in his seminal work, *Exit, Voice and Loyalty*. Hirschman's argument is that when an individual confronts an organization that is unresponsive to their concerns or needs, they have alternative ways of responding. They may simply refuse to participate further and leave (exit); they may protest in an attempt to change the system (voice); or they may attempt to work for change within the system (loyalty). Hirschman's key insight is that strong organizations are likely to be the most effective at resisting protest and attempts at internal change. The consequence of this is that they are the most vulnerable to exit. The weakness of strong organizations is precisely in their ability to resist change and the potential this creates for individuals to simply abandon it.

The concentric circle structure, that Elazar claims is descriptive of America's Jewish community, is a particularly strong organizational form. It contains successive layers of insiders and outsiders with strong norms, with respect to behavior and beliefs, that govern who is allowed to be at various distances from the center. This type of organizational form is particularly resistant to protest and internal change (though there has certainly been some of both). As a result, it should not be surprising that so many Jews have exited Jewish religious and communal life.

What is Herring's solution to this? He suggests that we adopt both in our thinking and practice a much more flexible model; what he and others have termed a network model of organization. The key idea here is that there is no longer any center and as a result there is also no unidimensional source of authority. People can participate in the network organization in a variety of ways and at different points. The network form of organization is the perfect form for our postmodern identities that consist of multiple selves and interests that only loosely cohere.

Although I agree with the thrust of Herring's recommendations, I am not sure that they do not create a new set of issues and problems. To investigate what these potentially might be, I want to suggest a parallel to the American Jewish community; the modern-day university. Both the American Jewish community and the modern university need to attract participants; lay people and congregants in the first case, students in the second. These are individuals who are, in some respects, customers who expect services and choices. In other respects, however, they need and expect to be among the "owners" of the institution. As a result, they expect to have a full voice in the institutional policy decision making and are expected to be contributing members to the institution. Furthermore, both types of institutions expect and are expected to teach and socialize their participants, but at the same time assume that their members will be active participants in organizational change. Finally, in part as a result of the above, both types of institutions have the classic issues about the balance of control between the professionals (faculty and administration) and the lay people (students).

The modern university long ago adopted a more flexible form. The concept of a liberal arts education where most courses were required and aimed at providing the student with a broad education is long gone. Although students today typically must have majors and often have to fulfill a set of distributional requirements, they are to a very great degree allowed to construct their own educations. Courses in Latin and Greek that were once required are seldom taken, and it is possible in most universities for a student to avoid taking all but a few courses that are related to his/her major. This trend has resulted in a host of books, typically by conservatives, who have decried this trend. Allan Bloom's *The Closing of the American Mind: How Higher Education Has Failed Democracy and Impoverished the Souls of Today's Students* and Dinesh D'Souza's *Illiberal Education: The Politics of Race and Sex on Campus* are perhaps the two most notable examples.

What have been the consequences of flexibility for American higher education? Certainly, in terms of numbers and dollars, it has been a great success. College enrollments are at an all time high. Brown University, once considered the "door mat" of the Ivy League, saw its applications soar when in the 1970s it dropped most of its formal requirements. Today, it is one of the most popular universities among top college students and competes for the very best against Harvard, Yale, and Princeton. Although tuition has outpaced inflation for several decades now, top institutions continue to receive record numbers of applicants. Harvard, whom one would have thought would have many years ago received all the best applicants, has seen the size of its applicant pool grow by 50 percent in the 1990s while the quality of its applicants has improved also. "Exit" certainly has not been a problem for higher education in the last couple of decades.

However, there is a darker side to this increased flexibility. Although it would take at least a full-length article if not a whole book to document this point, I want to suggest that in adopting a more flexible mode of operation, the university has also lost its central role within American public discourse. There was a time when the presidents of elite institutions (Pusey, Conant, Brewster, Hutchinson) were major public spokesmen on the critical issues of their day. This is no longer the case. More generally, universities were seen both as repositories of central cultural values and as institutions that not only taught, but socialized. The now quaint notion of a Harvard or Yale man embodies within it the idea that by going to a specific institution one acquired a particular set of values and even outlook on life. Arguably, universities were as much in the values business as they were part of the knowledge industry. This change has been in part due to universities first loosening and then severing their ties to the religious institutions and communities that found them. But of course, this is just part of the process by which they have acquired "flexibility."

How could increased "flexibility" have caused the changes I have described in the modern university? Let me return to Mary Douglas' book, *How Institutions Think*. Douglas argues that institutions think in ways analogous to the way individuals think. They have concepts, frameworks, beliefs systems, and the such, that determine how problems are approached and solved, how daily practice is carried out. In fact, Douglas argues that much individual thought is derivative of institutional thought. We think the way we do because of the institutions of which we are a part. It is often the institutional culture(s) that we are part of that provide the systems of thought, concepts, and frameworks we use in thinking through our own individual lives.

If institutions think, then how they think about some issues will almost certainly affect how they think about others. If universities decide that a highly flexible educational curriculum is desirable, then this will directly effect what these institutions have to say to the rest of the world about what is important and where our commitments should lie. Institutions, like people, can try to talk out of both sides of their mouths, but it is likely to be unpersuasive. More importantly, what institutions do will have major effects on what individuals will think of them. By almost any standard America has the most successful system of higher education in the world. Many would argue by a very wide margin. Yet the legitimacy and importance of America's higher education system has constantly been attacked in the last couple of decades. Much of this attack has centered around tuition increases that have consistently been higher than the inflation rate. But these attacks are often aimed at questioning whether higher education deserves its privileged position within American society whether in terms of the tax breaks or charity it receives, or more general its (past) vaulted moral position in American society. Between the lines, one can hear higher education's critics saying, "Why should, what are essentially trade schools, have the privileged positions they hold?"

I certainly do not want to argue that we should return to the American university of the past, though I do think it is important to recognize what has been lost as universities have changed. What I do want to argue is that the American university provides an important case study for the Jewish community. If universities think in the way that Mary Douglas means, then certainly religions do. In fact, the most important reference in her book is Emile Durkheim's *Elementary Forms of Religious Life*. Religion is first and foremost a way of thinking about the world.

We need to ask what are the consequences of having a Judaism, a Jewish communal life that is more "flexible" in form in which individuals and families connect in different ways? Reform Judaism in part provides an answer to this question. I will let the reader be the judge of Reform Judaism's success in this respect. But of course the kinds of changes that Rabbi Herring imagines are broader than that found in a single denomination. They have to do with Jewish communal life and how its is supported and enabled by Jewish religious and secular institutions. I am all for flexible, network organizations, if this means creating Jewish institutional structures that provide multiple points where Jews can acquire and wrestle with Jewish values and do so in a coherent fashion. I am much less sanguine about a Jewish life that results in what Bethamie Horowitz has called in her book, *Connections and Journeys: Assessing Critical Opportunities for Enhancing Jewish Identity*, "salad bar" Judaism. In becoming more flexible, in becoming more like network organizations, universities have lost a considerable portion of their ethnical and moral basis. It would be disastrous if Judaism and Jewish communal life were to befall the same fate.

References

Bloom, Allan D. 1988. *The Closing of the American Mind: How Higher Education Has Failed Democracy and Impoverished the Souls of Today's Students*. New York: Simon and Schuster.

D'Souza, Dinesh. 1991. *Illiberal Education: The Politics of Race and Sex on Campus*. New York: Free Press.

Douglas, Mary. 1986. *How Institutions Think*. Syracuse, NY: Syracuse University Press.

Durkheim, Emile. 2001. *Elementary Forms of Religious Life*. New York: Oxford University Press.

Elazar, Daniel J. 1995. *Community and Polity: The Organizational Dynamics of American Jewry.* Philadelphia: Jewish Publication Society.

Hirschman, Albert O. 1970. *Exit, Voice, and Loyalty*, Cambridge, MA: Harvard University Press.

Horowitz, Bethamie. 2000. *Connections and Journeys: Assessing Critical Opportunities for Enhancing Jewish Identity*. New York: United Jewish Appeal-Federation of New York.

Jonathan S. Woocher

Rabbi Hayim Herring's paper, *Judaism: A New Image for Understanding the Network Organization of American Jews*, reminds us once again that ideas and images, also have consequences. How we think about American Jewry, and even more, how we imagine it in our mind's eye, even sub-consciously, has a powerful impact on the policy choices we make and do not make. Rabbi Herring has done us all a great service in pointing out how one powerful image, that of American Jewry as a series of concentric circles marked by decreasing levels of Jewish commitment, all arrayed around an ostensibly magnetic core, has influenced, and perhaps skewed, much recent discussion about the Jewish future and policies that seek to ensure and enrich it. He has also opened up a new stage in that discussion by proposing an alternative image, that of organized Jewish life as a network, without any single center, that generates new possibilities both conceptually and practically in guiding Jewish policy making.

Let me state my criticisms at the outset: The paper as it stands is still clearly a work in progress. It seeks to encompass a great deal in a relatively few pages; everything from cutting-edge management theory to sociological analysis of the condition of contemporary American Jewry to prescriptions for organizational policies and practices. This is the paper's greatest strength and its weakness. In pulling together disparate threads drawn from several disciplines to help illuminate a vital issue in Jewish life, Rabbi Herring models a kind of wide-ranging, eclectic thinking that often produces striking new insights. At the same time, the paper is inevitably under-developed and lacking in rigor in certain key respects. For example, it does not fully analyze how the concentric circles/magnet metaphor has actually functioned in the organizational and policy arena, or even whether these two related, but not identical, images are always linked and equally pernicious. The paper also shifts back and forth in focus from the shape of American Jewry as a whole to how individual organizations are managed to implications for inter-organizational relationships in a way that is at times confusing. In the end, the network metaphor is not fully developed from either an analytical or a policy perspective. It stands, therefore, as a tantalizing alternative to the magnet metaphor, but not a powerful heuristic tool for recasting our understanding of what is to be done in ways that go beyond already widely discussed principles like starting where people are at, listening to our customers, and creating greater synergies and smoother hand-offs among institutions.

Having said this, it would indeed be a shame if this paper were set aside or given short shrift. The truth is that we badly do need new frameworks with which to imagine and think about American Jewish life and to shape our policy making and institutional practice. We have learned slowly, to give up, or at least to see as only partially true, a number of over-simplified and therefore misleading images of American Jews: e.g., that they are neatly divided between the affiliated and the unaffiliated; or, that they are readily arrayed along a spectrum from right to left, more to less, in terms of religiosity and Jewish commitment. Rabbi Herring has shown, convincingly for me, that the concentric circles/magnet metaphor indeed represents another limiting image that does not fit some of the facts of American Jewish life as we are learning about them from new research, or the latest thinking about how organizations thrive in a post-modern world. As with other such images, it is not a question of throwing this metaphor out altogether, we would lose some important insights were we to do so, but how to complement and supplement it with others that reveal what this one conceals.

In proposing the network as such a new metaphor, Rabbi Herring takes us, I believe, part way there. Networks today are frequently seen and studied as part of a larger class of phenomena called complex systems. Without going into all of the details of what complex systems are and how they work, I would suggest that we can draw on some of the rich imagery that has developed as scientists (both physical and social) have sought to describe such systems to take the network metaphor even farther and to begin to build a new imagistic language for talking about Jewish life today that will yield important insights for institutional and communal policy.

What are some of the images that help us to make sense of complex systems? The network is certainly one. But there are others. For example, complex systems are often depicted as landscapes upon which individual actors carry out their quests for the fundamental values that they seek (for a company, these might be high profits, market share, and an increasing stock price; for an individual, these might be meaning, connectedness to others in intimate community, and a sense of mastery over one's own life). Securing what one seeks requires climbing imagined peaks on this landscape; the higher the ground one attains, the more one is fulfilled in her/his quest. Now, imagine this landscape as complexity students do with many peaks (i.e., alternative potential sources of fulfillment in the quest for meaning, community, and mastery), some near at hand and familiar (the synagogue down the block), others farther away, but potentially higher. Now, imagine other journeyers/climbers on the landscape. They can help us reach the top, block our paths and draw us off in new directions. Imagine those already on various mountains. Are they carving out paths to ease the way to the top for others, or ignoring new climbers? Imagine us, all of us climbers: some of us like climbing in groups; some prefer to make our ascents solo; some want to tackle the highest mountains; others prefer easier climbs. Does this help us understand what is happening in Jewish life today, the multiple journeys taking place simultaneously, the choices confronting those on these journeys, and those who may or may not be in positions to facilitate them?

Or, change the image and imagine the mountains as ski resorts. For reasons that may or may not be evident, some resorts will become more popular than others. Their revenues will allow them to buy better snowmaking equipment, install larger and faster ski lifts, build more glamorous lodges, get more publicity and then even more people will come. (Complexity theorists would cite this as an illustration of the law of increasing returns.) Or, the initially popular resorts could get oppressively crowded; the familiar runs down the mountain could become boring and people will start drifting away. In a complex world, you cannot be sure which of these scenarios will come to pass (there is a lot that you cannot predict, especially on the individual scale) because people self-organize and everything evolves. (In fact, even the mountains are not stable; they too can grow taller or flatten out.) Not surprisingly, in the end we are likely to find that different people are going to different resorts (complexity theory would call each resort an attractor), some drawn by snow conditions, some by shorter lift lines, some by who else goes there (friends and family), all seeking, and some finding, a superior skiing experience.

And then, to round out our picture, we can bet that there will be some number of people who never leave the lodge, and others who really just want to get away on a cruise to the Caribbean and would not dream of going near the mountains (unless they happen to run into a really attractive person who is really into skiing). Do we recognize some of the features of Jewish life today in this image?

Enough metaphor (perhaps more than enough). The point is that different images of Jewish life (even somewhat far-fetched ones) *do* allow us to see phenomena that, as Rabbi Herring rightly asserts, more conventional ones, like the concentric circles/magnet metaphor, may cause us to miss.

Rabbi Herring argues that taking the concentric circles/magnet metaphor seriously allows us to see some of its inadequacies more clearly as we begin to ask tough questions about what the image implies. Is there really a center defined by the most intense Jewish commitment that provides the reference point for what we would like all Jews to be? Does the postulated magnetic pull of high intensity Jews and Jewish settings really work for all Jews? For some? Which ones? Under what conditions? (Others might argue that following this chain of questions demonstrates that the metaphor is in fact more valuable than Rabbi Herring credits; this is both an empirical and a normative judgment.) I would suggest that (whatever one may think of my mountains and ski resorts) images and metaphors that try to capture some of the insights of complexity theory about human systems including, but not limited to, the metaphor of a network, do have significant untapped potential for the contemporary American Jewish community. We need metaphors that help us to see the Jewish community as dynamic, evolving, and inter-connected, emerging as much from the bottom up as from the top down. We must understand that, like many organizations operating in complex environments today, it faces dual challenges. On the one hand, it tries to maintain its fundamental shape, its boundaries and identity, in the face of cross-cutting trends and uncertain courses of events; and, on the other, it seeks to adapt that shape with agility in order to encompass as many as possible of the multiple journeys taking place through and around the landscape it inhabits. Indeed, we are far from being a single set of concentric circles today, or from being able to thrive based on such an image.

So, my thanks to Rabbi Herring for opening up a much needed discussion. True to my own understanding, I would not dare to predict where this discussion will take us; how much of the old we will discard, how much of the new we will come to affirm, and vice versa. The important thing is to have the conversation, to try out new metaphors and to critique old ones. The game is on; let's go to it.

Alan Silverstein

As a practitioner, speaking directly from the grassroots of the Jewish community, I want to suggest that there are certain aspects of Hayim Herring's paper that I find useful and others that I find problematic. I very much agree that synagogues should provide easy access to information and be vision-driven, customer-sensitive, light on bureaucracy, high on ideas, less centrally driven, less turf oriented and find new ways to bring meaning into people's lives. My own metaphor is Rosenzweig's view that everyone is somewhere on the ladder of commitment. We should be non-judgmental, in that we validate everyone being somewhere on that infinite ladder or continuum of Jewish commitments. Everyone should be welcome to become involved in the Jewish community. Yet, on the other hand, there must be an expectation that we want to enable everyone to ascend the ladder at their own pace. After all, more Torah study is better than less. More prayer and ritual observance, *tzedakah*, expanded performance of acts of *hesed*, etc. is better than less. Plus, from my point of view, the ladder has three facets: Heart, Head and Hand. Certain Jews are best inspired at key times of their lives in terms of "Heart" (spiritual concerns)—prayer, ritual, meditative modes. Others are more receptive to "Head" (learning)—books, values, ideas, wisdom. Still others are "Hand" Jews —most comfortable doing deeds of loving kindness toward others or working on behalf of worthy Jewish institutions.

Meeting the ever-changing needs of individual Jews along such a diverse continuum mandates, as recommended by Hayim Herring, that synagogues ought to partner with JCCs and with federated agencies. For example, our local MetroWest (NJ) Federation has created a "Teen Initiative"—partnering with the JCC to find quality youth professionals, and to engage teens in synagogue youth groups as well as in adolescent programs at the Center and in the Federation system at large. Similarly, in MetroWest, synagogues will be implementing a new concept entitled "Metro Peers." Many congregants experience painful transitions and challenges in their lives—death of a loved one, serious illness, divorce, job loss, a child with learning disabilities or health challenges, and the frailty of elderly parents. JFS will train "Peers" who have been through such experiences to act as mentors and to offer a sympathetic ear. Numerous other partnering ventures are being implemented by our Jewish

Education Association, Jewish Vocational Service, Jewish Student Services, as well as other agencies.

On the problematic side, several aspects of Herring's thesis require further discussion. First, while I concur that the "core" ought not impose itself hierarchically from above, I suggest that there is a type of magnet effect that the "core" can have upon people on the periphery. This is especially true if the core is both healthy and open to receive newcomers. For example, when people come to my synagogue and are seeking a core of young families who are regular *shul* goers, or a *chevra* of day school families who attend with regularity, there is no doubt the presence of a viable and welcoming core group encourages newcomers to attend. So, too, in terms of Torah study. When people see successful professionals from our synagogue studying Talmud together at lunch hour in midtown Manhattan, this is a significant incentive to join the process. This does not mean that a core group ought to monopolize all decisions being made on behalf of the larger community, but a positive magnetic effect is both possible and desirable.

Second, when we speak about the vast "majority" of Jews being unaffiliated and unconnected, let us be careful with our definitions. At any point in time, over 40 percent of American Jews do belong to some synagogue. Moreover, during the course of their adult years, in most places in North America where Jews reside, in excess of 80 percent do join, at least in order to educate their children. The real issue for most rooted American Jews is not being unaffiliated but being under-affiliated during their membership years! Synagogues need help in conducting more effective in-reach to their marginal affiliates. The primary components of the hard core unaffiliated are clear: intermarried couples who are not raising their children as Jews, Jews in constant geographic or personal flux, empty nesters and retirees, Jews in dire economic straits embarrassed to ask for reduced fees, and immigrants from Russia, Israel and other cultures unfamiliar with affiliation. Each of these latter segments of the Jewish community requires additional forms of outreach. For the rest however, communal assistance in intensifying synagogal in-reach would be most cost and quality effective. Let us keep in mind that grassroots Jewish life in the twenty-first century is in synagogues and JCCs.

Third, I am worried that in Herring's model we may be encouraging people to remain isolated in their home or their computer terminal for accessing Jewish services. As Rabbi Harold Schulweis has asserted, "Jews need other Jews to be Jewish." There is something transformative about congregating with other Jews. In a related matter, Rabbi Lawrence Hoffman warns about abetting "the limited liability contract" relationship with an institution, in which the consumer merely purchases a specific service. Instead we need a more holistic relationship of Jews with their congregations. We need to provide for their needs, but also to benefit from their "gifts" of time and talent. When someone, like Allan Finkelstein, President of the JCCA, a major national Jewish agency and a participant in this symposium, joins my congregation and becomes the volunteer director of our High Holy Day Choir, our connection intensifies. Affiliation must be a two-way street. People feel much more invested in institutions in which they are "players."

Fourth, Herring's model of customizing Judaism to each person and family points the indispensable need to provide more staffing for congregations, JCCs and all institutions. This staffing need is critical if we truly seek to engage the diverse needs of twenty-first century Jews. We need to attract many more people into Jewish communal service of all types, especially since the ranks of Jewish professionals are graying. In MetroWest, for example, there is only one full-time worker serving the Jewish Singles population of 125,000 in three counties. The MetroWest JCC has only two full-time teen workers to meet the demands of thousands of Jewish adolescents. Synagogues in particular are notoriously understaffed, lacking family educators, program directors, social workers and other skilled personnel.

Fifth, there is the wisdom of Laurence R. Iannaccone's famous analysis of why liberal churches struggle (American Journal of Sociology, March 1994, 1180–1211). He suggests that they often err by demanding little in the way of separation from society-at-large. Rather than regarding every level of Jewish action or inaction as equally meritorious, let us remember something powerful that stems from non-coercive group expectations elevating and inspiring the level of involvement of others. For example, Rabbi Eric Yoffee of the Union of American Hebrew Congregations (Reform) is urging liberal Jews of his movement to inspire one another to read Jewish books, to pray together more frequently, and to incorporate *mitzvot* into their temple and private lives. Similarly, in my Conservative synagogue's Shabbat morning *chevra*, there is a pattern of young families inspiring one another. Most send their children to Jewish summer camp. While newcomers at any level of involvement are welcomed joyfully into our ranks, this expectation informally filters into their lives. The result is quite evident in the mushrooming attendance of our members at Ramah day and overnight camps. This effect is true as well in terms of burgeoning numbers attending Jewish Day Schools. A similar rise in observance of Kashrut and other commitments to Jewish observance is also evident. The total absence of informal (non-coercive) expectations is not a benefit.

In sum, I applaud much of the thrust of Hayim Herring's stimulating paper as a supplementary model to that of Daniel Elazar, qualified by these cautionary points:

- Jewish life must be mobile and flexible and open to meeting new challenges, but it ought not relinquish all traditionalist perspectives; all sense of boundaries.

- Ascending the ladder of commitments is preferable to standing static or diminishing one's involvement as a Jew.

- Congregating with other Jews has a tangible power that ought to be encouraged.

- Funding for additional staffing is critical.

- The existence of certain communal expectations is a benefit that should not be abandoned.

- Core groups can have a positive magnetic impact upon Jews on the periphery.

- Let us focus our efforts upon improving the rate of success in working with the under-affiliated at synagogues and JCCs. They represent the overwhelming percentage of Jews who are both receptive to greater engagement yet are "at risk" of falling back into indifference and non-involvement.

Allan Finkelstein

Those who know me are aware that Hayim Herring's basic premise is one that totally supports my belief that our communities need a new way of thinking about how we approach serving Jews. Communities need to know how to work and how to work together. There are two specific areas of interest to me: 1) how we relate to members/participants and 2) how the institutions relate to each other. Here are a few comments about what I think is important in this paper:

I absolutely believe that the time for the "magnet" metaphor is behind us. The core/periphery distinction is far too black and white to accurately reflect the reality of where most American Jews are today. We (Jewish agencies) have, for too long, been thinking in terms of "what I need and what I want."

True, the real "core" active, involved Jews are exactly as Elazar described them. But they are far from being the challenge for us, and far from being the majority. The core model does not work. Jews are affiliated today in different ways at different times in their lives. They do not think institutionally like we might want them to. This is a flaw in how the American Jewish community works. We work against the consumer mentality that is very real. Hayim Herring says, "individual Jews who do not meet the criteria of institutional involvement may actually lead rich Jewish lives." This is important. We have been judging Jews based on affiliation and if they belong to what we think is important. They might have rich Jewish lives that we do not recognize. He quotes Sales and Tobin who say that "affiliation is not tantamount to religiosity." Jews think about meeting their needs in the best, most convenient way that is available at the time that they need it. What they think is convenient at one time may not be how our communities have structured themselves. I agree with Herring that business analogies are valid and real. When dealing with consumers, they are only going to buy a service if it is good. If our services are not of quality, Jews will go elsewhere.

Where we fail as a community is that we still work very much in institutional "silos" and we use language of exclusivity and competition, rather than of collaboration and community. We "talk" community, but we do not act like community. We are constantly using language that badmouths other institutions. Herring notes that "institutional policies around involvement assume a permanent, stable, physical address" for those who may not be thinking in those terms. We also assume long term affiliation with a given institution. I think a vision of a strong synagogue is still at the core of everything. But a strong synagogue without a strong community around it is weak.

We know, as Hayim Herring points out, that the younger generations are skeptical about allegiance. We know that loyalty to organizations is no longer the norm. The days of joining the JCC, the synagogue, or giving to the federation because that is "just what you do" are not there anymore. We have a real opportunity to build loyalty to community, if only we can get our act together to think about the totality of community as a system that impacts the Jewish journey of the individual.

The network model is an effective way to do this if we realize that people want more than one way to do it. We must think about the totality of the community as a system that impacts the "Jewish journey" of the individual.

While I do not buy the network model totally as it plays out in the paper, I do congratulate Hayim Herring on giving us a real and challenging basis for redesigning how we work. What I believe works for me in his model is the following:

- The interdependence requires that all aspects of community feed "data" or individuals to each other as we understand their needs and see that, perhaps, another institution or experience is more appropriate. We do not do that now. We only worry about serving people when they are in our institution. Wherever the individual enters Jewish life, we have to help them get to the rest of the network. We are bad at that because we do not have the right language or the right attitude.

- The idea that there cannot be a "command control" central to meet the needs of today's Jews. Institutions are critical, indeed I represent one of them, but the ability for each to be entry points to the other is a critical notion. Personalized service and quick response have not been hallmarks of our organizations. Just because we are responsive to somebody's needs and we bring them in an effective way, does not mean that we do not care about

quality. We have to train our staff and lay leaders very differently so that when we bring someone in, we bring them into a network. I know that some people view this as losing institutional
strength and quality of involvement. I believe the opposite, that
a quality experience in one institution when combined with a
customer-friendly response to the individual, will, in the end
build closer ties to whole community if we are all articulating
the communal message. That is a big "if." A recent study in
Boston showed that on every measure of Jewish identification,
those who have multiple affiliations score higher. If you belong
to only one institution, your level of Jewish involvement will
tend to be lower. Therefore, anyone who says that one specific
Jewish organization is the total answer is wrong.

- The characterization of a model that focuses on "planning, organizing, leading and coordinating," rather than controlling, certainly would lead to a more meaningful collaborative approach.
  The control model is just not working; it really turns people off.
  The question is whether or not we can let go of years of tradition
  and "built up" ways of working.

I would suggest that, at a minimum, we consider the "network" idea
as a new way of thinking together, and planning. If we immediately move
to tear apart the details or some of the examples that Hayim Herring provides, we may actually never get to discover the potential of the bigger
picture that he is painting. Let us take the following as challenges:

- The idea that the individual "journey" through Jewish life is a valid
  concept that is worth exploring.

- The idea that not everything must radiate from one "address" or "central" core.

- That we are richer as a system than as individual institutions.

I would add that a different "language" can be created, one that is supportive of other institutions and that assists people in moving more comfort-
ably between them. Jews seek multiple communities, not just one, the his-
toric community of Eastern Europe. There are many different communities,
and they must relate to each other. These ideas could form the basis of a meaningful dialogue that would begin to test some of Hayim Herring's ideas.

Neuman F. Pollack

Rabbi Herring has addressed a central issue confronting the American Jewish organizational community. The dilemma being faced is how to reconcile the reality of patterns of Jewish cohesiveness in contemporary American society with existing organizational structures. One could argue that the traditional religious and social needs of individuals in the Jewish community have not changed; what has changed is the expression and satisfaction of those needs.

The Jewish community in the Diaspora organized itself around institutions designed to promote group identity and group cohesion. Members of the *community* supported and remained loyal to its institutions because of the perceived benefits they offered. Group theory purports that people adhere to groups for a variety of reasons, the most basic and pervasive of which deals with individual and group survival. The institutions defined by the group provide security in the face of opposition and other external threats to their existence; i.e., there is *power* in numbers. Organizations representing group interests are viewed as essential to the achievement of goals on behalf of the community. Furthermore, group affiliation provides individuals with mechanisms for social (and economic and political) gains in the context of the broader society. Lastly, participation (and for some mere membership) in the affairs of such groups serves to fulfill individual needs of status and self-esteem.

If the underlying identity of the group sets members apart from the broader society, the institutions of the group that develop serve to define, legitimize and, indeed, ensure their continued existence. Thus, a dispersed Jewish community first organized institutions to define its boundaries, as well as to protect and defend its existence in the broader society in which it found itself. This is true both in terms of religious and non-religious needs. The stronger the perception of threat from the society beyond, the more coherent the boundary and the stronger the institutions. Indeed, if the threat became too severe (and adequately acknowledged) the *community* could remove itself geographically from the threat. The historical roots of the Zionist movement and the waves of immigration to the United States emanate from this orientation. In the twentieth century the Holocaust proved to be an unprecedented threat that both severely disrupted, yet hastened relocation and boundary setting for the worldwide Jewish community culminating in the establishment of the State of Israel.

A wondrous, yet curious phenomenon developed in the United States. The fundamental philosophy of the American republic promulgated tolerance of religion and social origins of its people. To be sure, such tolerance and broad acceptance of immigrant Jews (and other minorities) was slow to build; social acceptance continues to evolve. However, the pace has quickened in the post World War II era for the American Jewish community, as well as African-American, Hispanic-American, and other ethnic and cultural groups. The pace of such change, while refreshing, desirable and laudable, has had an impact upon the very institutions of the affected groups, which for so long worked both to define and protect their members and lessen the boundaries themselves.

A quarter of a century ago Daniel Elazar presented a view of the American Jewish community that was both reflective of the "reality on the ground," and efficacious in describing its inner workings. The "magnet metaphor" was accepted and served well as a descriptive theme because it did not challenge the "reality on the ground," nor did it require the American Jewish community or its institutions to modify their behavior in order to fit the model. To be sure, not all Jewish individuals or Jewish institutions adhered perfectly to the metaphor, but its broad-based acceptance, as noted by Rabbi Herring, served to stifle competing views.

As noted, the pace of social change in the United States has accelerated in the post World War II period. Significant progress in social integration occurred in the 1950's and 1960's, much to the credit of Jewish institutions that fought for and supported the softening, if not outright elimination, of social, economic, and political boundaries. A generation of leaders schooled during the threatening days of the inter-war period would remain in control of religious and social institutions into the 1970's and 1980's. The institutions and inter-institutional relationships would, therefore, remain largely unchallenged and unchanged, even as the social fabric was rapidly being altered. The Elazar metaphor was elegant in its simplicity and highly reflective of the *community* he was studying.

Though underlying threats to Jewish survival in the United States were diminishing, worldwide issues of Jewish survival were not. With well-developed institutions in place, the energies and efforts of the American Jewish community could be directed toward the bolstering of the State of Israel, advocacy on behalf of Soviet Jewry, the fighting of anti-Jewish terrorism, and relocation of Ethiopian Jews, among other issues. Again, with threats defined externally, that is, as emanating from beyond the community's boundary, strong institutions, organized to support and protect the good of the greater group, were essential for success. Few in the organized American Jewish community recognized the fundamental changes that were occurring in the broader society that would impact the fabric of Jewish life in America; fewer still sounded a clarion call to action.

What was occurring in the post-modern era of late twentieth century America was a major exodus across the Jewish boundary into the mainstream of the American society. It was not that Jews were renouncing their Jewishness, *per se*, rather, it was a rapid inter-generational shift away from being defined by one's Jewishness and the need to self-actualize through Jewish institutions to being defined by one's *humanness* and the satisfaction of social needs in the broader marketplace of institutions including, but not exclusively limited to traditional Jewish ones. In a word, it was *safe* to be Jewish in America and move beyond the safety of the *community* and its protective institutions. Indeed, this has lead to the challenge facing these institutions—their very survival. Of course, one could also argue that this poses a threat to Jewish survival in America in the sense of its cohesiveness and unifying sense of purpose.

This post-modern era is characterized by fragmentation of interests. It is also characterized by *anomie*—an antiseptic rootlessness in society. Diversity is the "buzz word" affecting both business and social institutions in the American society. Not only are existing organizational structures attempting to transform themselves to reflect this diversity, but also new institutions are being formed to cater to the needs of smaller subsets of society. Such changes are reflected in the business community, as well as non-business entities.

The Elazar magnet metaphor did not suggest that there was no diversity in the American Jewish community, rather, it suggested that the strength of identification and support of the institutions was derived from a highly committed core, or cadre, of individuals. The institutions served those on the periphery, to the extent they sought service, but were not essential to the survival of the institutions. Institutional survival was assured by recruitment of new people into the core. As long as there was a perceived external threat, institutions were able to maintain themselves. The threat today, as aptly described by Hayim Herring, is from within the Jewish community, which is no longer defined exclusively by a perceived external threat.

The problem is one of redefining goals and organizational rationales, as well as marketing and delivering desired programs and services to members of a Jewish community that has moved beyond the group boundary. The challenge is to bring about change in the very institutions, that helped to foster the fundamental changes, that have occurred in the broader community. But herein lies the dilemma: how to bring about this type of institutional change to reflect the newly articulated needs of the American Jewish community that has a plethora of options open to it.

Herring suggests that it is time to move beyond the Elazar magnet metaphor to a more efficacious network matrix model of Jewish community institutions. The underlying theory, relying as it does on a business organizational perspective, is proscriptive. It takes advantage of developments in technology and telecommunications and it recognizes the emerging spatial distribution patterns of the American Jewish population. However, unlike the Elazar magnet metaphor, which was reflective of the "reality on the ground," the Herring network metaphor is yet to be evidenced in reality. That is not to say that it is not efficacious, nor to say that it could not succeed in preserving a sense of Jewish community in the American society.

Hayim Herring recognizes this dilemma. He seeks to illustrate how the network metaphor could serve as a guideline to preserve the new American Jewish community. As his example of how the network metaphor might operate illustrates, it is not the Jewish individual who must change; it is the function, structure and orientation of Jewish institutions, that must change. But people and institutions are resistant to change due to fear of losing influence and control, uncertainty and ambiguity surrounding the direction change may take, and a general lack of faith regarding the wisdom of change. Added to these factors is a denial that there is even a problem that needs to be addressed. Those individuals who are at the core (of the Elazar magnet) are fiercely committed to existing policies and organizational structures. They are dismissive of cries for change since they do not believe the fundamental purposes of their organizations are no longer worthy goals to be pursued.

The example of how the Herring network metaphor might operate is clearly developed and includes the most salient of issues facing the American Jewish community today. However, it misses a central point, which would bolster the case it attempts to illustrate: namely, strengthening the bond of Jewishness in a community increasingly characterized by its success, mobility, and assimilation. A young family with a non-Jewish partner residing in an exurban diverse community does need to be connected to the Jewish community, and does pose a particular problem that can be solved, in part, through "network Judaism." It is more likely, however, to be solved by new institutions, since few existing organizations have shown the willingness to engage in networking to the extent portrayed by this example.

Perhaps more compelling for the future of the Jewish community and its institutions would be the example of a more "traditional" family living in an urban or suburban setting confronting the pressures of coping with success, mobility, and assimilation in the first instance so that its members can make both a successful transition into the modern society and remain attached to the Jewish community at the same time. Why is this example more illustrative of how "network Judaism" could work? Simply because the leaders of traditional Jewish institutions will be better able to relate to it. It would appeal to their sense of community survival—their traditional modus operandi.

In reality, both examples, and others unstated, are important; but that is beside the point. The focal point of our discussion should be how to energize traditional institutions to adopt new missions and goals; to undergo structural re-engineering; to become more consumer oriented meeting the needs of an increasingly diverse American Jewish community. Dr. Herring's provocative paper on "network Judaism" is important for raising the issue and challenging the status quo ante of the Elazar magnet metaphor.

Reply and Policy Recommendations

Hayim Herring

An observation in the Talmud (Ta'anit 7a) notes that disciples of the wise sharpen one another through analytic discussions of *halakha* (Jewish law). In that tradition, I wish to thank my colleagues for their incisive responses. They helped me to identify both the weaknesses and the strengths of my proposed model for understanding and enhancing Jewish community. I gratefully accept some parts of their critique, while continuing to disagree with others. The following thoughts are reflections and reactions to some of the issues that they raised.

Barry Shrage has done a marvelous job illustrating how suitable a network model is for federations. His remarks are poetic and pragmatic, giving the United Jewish Community system both food for thought in developing a renewed sense of purpose and a framework for thinking about that purpose. He reminds those in the federation world that "meeting emerging needs" was the impulse that initially gave birth to federations, and that fundraising was the vehicle through which those needs were met. That purpose of "meeting emerging needs" is as relevant today as it was over one hundred years ago. However, using a network orientation allows for meeting a new, unimagined, and perhaps unprecedented set of needs.

Nevertheless, I do disagree with him on several issues. He speaks about the absence of community in contemporary life and the yearning that people have for it. Connecting Jewish individuals to community can be a powerful antidote to high rates of mobility. However, I do not assume, as he does, that Jewish individuals and their families in all their diversity will experience a feeling of being "at home" in the Jewish community. To the contrary, many may have to be persuaded that the Jewish community is a place where they will be welcomed. While institutional and communal strategies on outreach should be built on the strength and beauty that a Jewish community can offer, they should not presuppose that individuals will automatically associate an "at home" feeling with the Jewish community.

Additionally, I believe that Barry Shrage has too exclusive a view of the importance of Torah and learning for the creation of community. I agree that these are exceptional vehicles, when used well, for achieving this goal, but, Jewish culture, broadly defined in all of its ancient and contemporary richness, can create equally strong communal experiences. A community that only emphasizes learning without culture is destined to reach a limited population in an equally limiting way. Torah reaches the head; culture can touch the heart. We need to think about how to expand our repertoire beyond learning to include cultural experiences so that people can be inspired to live Jewishly and imagine what it means to have a transcendent vision of Jewish life.

Finally, while Shrage acknowledges the importance of including innovative Jewish grassroots organizations in the networked community, I am concerned about his emphasis on synagogues and JCC's as "gateway" institutions. They definitely are worthy of intensified communal funding as they are an important component of the infrastructure of the existing organized community, but, we also need to develop a mentality of investing in innovative, start-up, grassroots organizations. Federations have an interesting role to play in supporting existing organizations without neglecting emerging organizations that are engaging difficult-to-reach populations, and helping new organizations without arousing the anxiety of existing organizations.

David Gordis cautions those that embrace the network metaphor to remember that Jewish institutions remain authentic only when they speak from "the values of Jewish tradition." At the same time, he recognizes clearly that given the influence that organizational metaphors exert, they must reflect the "tectonic shifts in Jewish life." Some individuals will rush to embrace the new network metaphor; others will rally to defend the old core-periphery model. I believe that David Gordis offers wise counsel in suggesting that greater insight about the nature of Jewish community today will emerge from struggling to embrace new metaphors while not relinquishing those parts of older ones that help us maintain our authenticity.

Christopher Winship observed that, even in this fledging form, a network metaphor, like all new "solutions," produces a new set of "problems." His cautionary analogy suggesting the loss of the university's ability to transmit a set of values merits serious consideration. After all, the primary "business" of the Jewish community is values, vision, and meaning. In arguing for flexibility and inclusivity, I do not wish to create the impression that all is permitted! Indeed, in a network framework, the exercise of leadership and the articulation of a compelling Jewish vision supported by Jewish values and behaviors becomes more important than ever precisely because of the concerns that Prof. Winship raises.

Jonathan Woocher is an individual with tremendous insights and sensitivities about the Jewish community. His observations regarding the lack of actionable policy recommendations are in order, and I have included a preliminary list of policy recommendations following this response section. Where I disagree with him is in his preference to put network organizations in a broader framework of complex adaptive systems. I believe that this is undesirable for several reasons.

Complexity theory is a useful descriptive tool for understanding how organizations function and relate to one another. In particular, the role of "butterfly effects," transforming feedback, attention to boundaries, and founding principles as generators of organizations are important concepts in analyzing organizations. However, complex adaptive systems theory is limiting in two respects: its name is apt, for it is difficult to explain; and, it tends to produce policy statements and programmatic recommendations of a most general nature. Any framework that is not easily grasped will be of scant utility. However, as we are in need of multiple metaphors about community, it is worth investigating what aspects of complex adaptive systems may have specific application for the Jewish community.

I take issue with Jonathan Woocher on the ability of the network metaphor to provide both a coherent descriptive and prescriptive perspective. My paper is certainly not the definitive and comprehensive statement on the applicability of network theory for the Jewish community. As he properly notes, it is really the opening of a dialogue. However, network organization analysis has been applied to a diverse array of fields, including entertainment, publishing, auto manufacturing, government, and biotechnology. It is a well-developed field with an extensive literature. One of my hopes in writing this paper was to bring this framework to the attention of communal policy makers, planners and programmers, and I look forward to expanding this preliminary thinking in the future.

As a former pulpit rabbi, I have much empathy for the concerns that Rabbi Silverstein raises. As noted by Jonathan Woocher as well, I may not be giving enough credence to the magnetic attraction that institutions can exert on their members, but I also know that magnets, under certain conditions, repel with equal strength. We need to understand better under what conditions institutions exert a pull and why at other times they exert a push. For example, this pull effect seems to be strongest for families with children up to the years of Bar/Bat Mitzvah. Thinking about the developmental needs of adults as they mature, perhaps there are new ways for institutions to assert their magnetic pull after these years. Moreover, we need to better understand how institutions can be positioned to exert a magnetic pull for the many individuals who never fall into this cohort.

Fundamentally, Rabbi Silverstein and I appear to read the Jewish community differently (or, perhaps we are each viewing a different part of the Jewish community). Rabbi Silverstein evokes Rosenzweig's image of a "ladder of commitment" and divides the community between the "affiliated" and "hard core unaffiliated." Again, these are linear, judgmental images and terms that do not sufficiently capture the dynamic journeys that individuals embark upon and their reluctance to accept *a priori* institutional demands. These are the kinds of terms and images that read many Jews (perhaps anywhere from sixty to seventy-five percent) out of the community. My own experience is that we can gain the same commitments to a Jewish way of life with a different and more inclusive set of terms and images.

I also believe that Rabbi Silverstein misconstrues the expanded role that I envision for technology. I do not believe that virtual community is a replacement for real-time, face-to-face community; instead, it is a complement to it that can create enriched relationships and connections-between individuals, and between individuals and institutions. An analogy with the telephone can illustrate this point. The telephone did not replace the need for face-to-face meeting, but strengthened existing relationships and made new ones possible.

At the same time, we need to be open to the emergence of new forms of community, even ones like on-line communities. As technology improves, and it becomes routine to talk into a computer and view a person at the other end of the terminal, some of the concerns about depersonalization will decrease.

The issue of affiliation and the percentages of those who are formally "affiliated" with an institution is not my primary concern. The important question for me (as I suspect it is for Rabbi Silverstein) is, rather, asking how institutions are building Jewish lives and community. Clearly, given the variable and generally low rate of synagogue (25%-40%) and other institutional affiliation, we have more work to do in placing the existing resources of institutions (and new ones) at the disposal of individuals who are in search of community. Perhaps, then, Rabbi Silverstein's assertion of "grassroots Judaism" being lived in synagogues and Jewish Community Centers will become more of a reality.

Allan Finkelstein's remarks are both precise and concise. Perhaps this model resonates well for him because Jewish Community Centers are the nexus between individuals of all ages and other Jewish community institutions. As such, they frequently hear the frustrations expressed by both of these sides of the Jewish community equation: individuals and institutions. An endorsement of the basic framework of this model by someone with his perspective lends even more urgency, in my mind, to explore it further. I also appreciate the suggestion that new thinking about community must be supported by new language that expresses its concepts.

Neuman Pollack provides a very insightful analysis of the persistence of the Elazar magnet model. He notes that compelling threats to Jewish group survival fostered the creation of strong institutions, that in turn helped to reinforce clearly demarcated boundaries between the Jewish community and the broader community. However, as he observes, there has been a "major exodus across the Jewish boundary into the mainstream of American society." The only way for existing institutions to recover a role in the life of Jewish individuals is to redefine their function, structure and orientation. Clearly, I agree with him on this essential point.

Pollack suggests that many or even most existing Jewish institutions may not be capable of such a redefinition. Instead, he hints that the new realities of contemporary Jewish life may need to be satisfied through the creation of new institutions. Ultimately he may be proven correct, but I am not ready to concede this point at the present time. With the many change efforts underway aimed at synagogues, JCC's, and other bedrock institutions, there may be considerable reason for hoped-for change occurring within these institutions. As a strategy, we need to invest intelligently both in existing and emerging institutions.

The writing of this paper in itself has illustrated to me the power of a network framework. My colleagues, incredibly generous with their time and insights, came from diverse fields: synagogues, universities, federations, educational organizations, foundations, Jewish Community Centers-and more. I also heard from others who received pre-publication copies that enriched this document with their critique. Dr. David Gordis and Rabbi Zachary Heller of the Wilstein Institute in true network fashion coordinated but did not control its development. Through several real-time forums and virtual electronic discussions, they have provided a constructive network model of debate through the Wilstein Institute of Jewish Policy Studies that enriches the Jewish community. For this, I offer my deep appreciation.

Policy Recommendations

In keeping with the spirit of this paper, I believe that meaningful policy recommendations can only be developed on the local level, for each community has its own unique characteristics. However, I offer these ideas as suggestions for starting a conversation around the issues raised by "Network Judaism" that hopefully will occur in many communities, or for accelerating a conversation that I know has already begun in others. I have organized these recommendations around the four challenges raised for institutions in implementing the network model.

Jewish institutions should consider actively pursuing a marketing strategy that is appropriate to their particular setting. Marketing involves much more than the use of clever advertisements to draw people to an activity. Building relationships with individuals is at the heart of a true marketing strategy. In other words, marketing is both a mentality and a process that permeates every aspect of an organization.

How would an organization that pursued a marketing strategy behave? To begin with, it would have membership policies that were tailored to the different stages of life of its potential members. Given that there are four generations of potential members alive today, each with a different attitude toward institutions, policies would differ for each age cohort and for different family constellations (from single people to blended families that may include Jewish and non-Jewish children). Additionally, programs and services offered by institutions would be informed by knowledge of human development and Jewish identity formation. This last point is critical, as it is no longer possible for institutions to develop relationships with the people that it hopes to serve without understanding their human and Jewish developmental needs.

Institutions would develop ongoing methods for seeking feedback from their members about the programs and services that they offer. They would then use that information to shape (discard, recreate or invent) programs and services on a regular basis. They would also use multiple media formats to communicate with their constituents (interactive electronic, print, cable television and radio), and customize information based on their target audience. Marketing, in this regard, can be thought of as one form of organizational learning.

Of course, this kind of reorientation would involve a retraining of staff and volunteer leadership to work more closely as a team. No single individual can be expected to know or learn about its constituents. That is really the responsibility of staff and volunteer leadership. Psychologists, educators, rabbis, individuals with expertise in marketing, and technology specialists need to work as a team and examine how best to learn about and serve their target community within their mission. Specifically, staff and volunteer training in the area of marketing, working in collaboration, psychology, organizational dynamics and Jewish identity formation would be helpful.

Jewish institutions should consider increasing their internal communications capacity. Taking the time and making the effort to learn about members is important, but that information has to be shared so that all appropriate staff can use it. Having worked in and with many different institutions, my impression is that internal organizational communications often can be best characterized as sporadic. Using a large synagogue as an example, the youth, religious school and adult education programs often function independently of one another, despite the fact that children and their parents in these programs often overlap. Thus, staff and volunteers may have knowledge about an adult learner that could be useful in planning a youth group or religious school activity where a parent could volunteer his or her talents; or, a rabbi may neglect to communicate with a youth worker about a family problem that a teen is experiencing.

These are merely illustrations of the often low level of internal communications that are detrimental to an organization effectively serving its members. Technology can help to enhance internal communications, and can be an important complement to regular, real-time meetings. However implemented, ongoing, systemic communications about members are necessary to maintain current members and attract new ones.

Jewish institutions should considering forming networks with other Jewish institutions that have complementary strengths. At the risk of restating the obvious, given the complexity and diversity of the Jewish community, and the resources required to meet their attendant challenges, no single institution can fulfill the array of Jewish needs that exist today. Here are a few networking questions for consideration:

a. Within legal and moral bounds, why cannot more institutions share information about members that they have in common so that volunteer talent in one institution can become involved in other institutions?

b. Why do not more joint membership, marketing and program-ming packages exist, especially targeting those that are less like-ly to be involved in Jewish communal institutions?

c. Why cannot local joint professional and volunteer continuing education programs be developed?

d. Why cannot institutions share staff and "out source" programs and services to other institutions?

Jewish institutions should consider forming networks with other institutions outside of the Jewish community that offer com-plementary programs and services. It is probably only a slight exag-geration to suggest that most for-profit and many non-profit organiza-tions routinely seek to expand their market share. For many reasons, the Jewish community is an attractive market. Universities, hospitals, law firms, cultural institutions, and retail stores (these are just some exam-ples) present wonderful opportunities for networking. (In fact, this is a strategy that we have pursued successfully in Minneapolis, as have other communities.) Jewish social, cultural, recreational and educational oppor-tunities can be made more accessible to Jewish individuals through such networks.

These sample policy recommendations are not revolutionary. However, taken as a package, they can help turn a new way of thinking about community into an action plan. This volume of essays and respons-es is the beginning of a stimulating discussion that we hope will be joined by its readers.